Cambridge El<

Elements in Public Economics
edited by
Robin Boadway
Queen's University
Frank A. Cowell
The London School of Economics and Political Science
Massimo Florio
University of Milan

ECONOMIC PRINCIPLES
OF COMMODITY
TAXATION

Vidar Christiansen
University of Oslo

Stephen Smith
University College London

CAMBRIDGE
UNIVERSITY PRESS

CAMBRIDGE
UNIVERSITY PRESS

University Printing House, Cambridge CB2 8BS, United Kingdom

One Liberty Plaza, 20th Floor, New York, NY 10006, USA

477 Williamstown Road, Port Melbourne, VIC 3207, Australia

314–321, 3rd Floor, Plot 3, Splendor Forum, Jasola District Centre, New Delhi – 110025, India

79 Anson Road, #06–04/06, Singapore 079906

Cambridge University Press is part of the University of Cambridge.

It furthers the University's mission by disseminating knowledge in the pursuit of education, learning, and research at the highest international levels of excellence.

www.cambridge.org
Information on this title: www.cambridge.org/9781009002028
DOI: 10.1017/9781009004497

© Vidar Christiansen and Stephen Smith 2021

First published 2021

A catalogue record for this publication is available from the British Library.

ISBN 978-1-009-00202-8 Paperback
ISSN 2516-2276 (online)
ISSN 2516-2268 (print)

Economic Principles of Commodity Taxation

Elements in Public Economics

DOI: 10.1017/9781009004497
First published online: March 2021

Vidar Christiansen
University of Oslo

Stephen Smith
University College London

Author for correspondence: Vidar Christiansen, vidar.christiansen@econ.uio.no

Abstract: The authors provide a broad overview of economic aspects of commodity taxation, focussing in particular on theory and on policy applications in OECD countries. Some major papers in public economics have discussed whether these taxes should be levied at a uniform rate, or whether different commodities should be taxed differently, for reasons of either equity or efficiency. The authors begin with this question, and then discuss further issues, including the economic incidence of commodity taxes, the properties of the VAT, the taxation of financial services, the international aspects of commodity taxation, and environmental and health policy aspects.

Keywords: Value added tax, sales taxes, social efficiency and distribution, behavioural effects of taxation, international aspects of tax policy, taxation of financial services

ISBNs: 9781009002028 (PB), 9781009004497 (OC)
ISSNs: 2516-2276 (online), 2516-2268 (print)

Contents

Preface

Commodity taxation – by which we mean, broadly speaking, taxes levied on the sale of goods and services – forms a substantial part of the revenue-raising resources of most governments. Across the OECD countries as a whole, taxes on the sale of goods and services accounted for about one third of all tax revenues in 2017, the overwhelming proportion of which came from a large general tax on the sale of goods and services. In nearly all OECD countries, with the notable exception of the United States, this general tax on sales took the form of a value added tax (VAT), a tax which has spread world-wide over the past sixty years.

The design and structure of commodity taxation has for many years been an active field of both theoretical and empirical research in public economics. In this Element we provide an overview of the major economic issues highlighted by this research, focussing mainly on theoretical issues, and on policy in OECD countries. Section 1 defines the scope of the subject: what, precisely, do we mean by commodity taxation? In Section 2 we sketch the outlines of the economic literature on the optimal structure of commodity taxes. When would uniform taxation of all goods and services be optimal, in the sense of minimizing the excess burden of tax revenue raising, or achieving the socially optimal balance between efficiency and equity? Section 3 discusses the incidence of indirect taxes: who ultimately bears the burden of these taxes? Section 4 discusses the design and properties of the VAT, and Section 5 discusses the particular issues involved in the application of VAT or other sales taxes to financial services. Section 6 discusses international aspects of commodity taxation, including the effects of border tax adjustments on traded goods, the effects of cross-border shopping, and tax exporting. Section 7 looks at the use of commodity taxes to achieve behavioural change, such as in environmental and health policy. Section 8 discusses a number of other issues in the recent literature, and Section 9 highlights some promising directions for future research.

1 Introduction and Overview

Commodity taxes have a long history. Taxes on the production, movement, or sale of certain commodities have for many years been a significant source of state revenues in many countries. In a system without modern accounting conventions, and with limited administrative capacity, the production or movement of commodities provided an observable basis for levying taxes, with a rough-and-ready relationship to citizens' ability to pay. Only in the last century or so have taxes on income overtaken taxes on commodities and on real property as the most powerful revenue instruments available to government.

The long history of taxing commodities left its imprint on the tax systems in many countries well into the twentieth century, in the form of patterns of commodity taxation which reflected the accretion over time of excises and other taxes on particular commodities. Even today, traces of the past can be found, in the form of special taxes or tax exemptions for particular commodities, with no apparent justification other than policy inertia. However, the second half of the twentieth century saw quite dramatic changes in commodity taxation, in particular with the development and spread of broad-based taxes such as VAT that replaced many older commodity taxes with a more considered and coherent system and structure.

The contribution that economics can make to rational and efficient commodity tax policy is the underlying theme of this short Element.

Before turning to the various aspects of commodity taxation that economic research has analysed, we begin by drawing some boundaries to the scope of our analysis, by looking at the definition of our subject matter, and the types of taxation with which we will be concerned. We have had to be selective, and have left out some interesting topics, simply because there is not space to do them justice.

By commodity taxes we generally mean taxes on the sale of commodities, in other words, the sale of goods and services.[1] These can include sales to consumers – retail sales – and also sales of intermediate goods between businesses. The literature also refers to commodity taxes as consumption taxes, where the perception is that the taxes in question are taxes on consumption goods rather than intermediate inputs to production or investment goods. We shall use these more or less close synonyms interchangeably, but will be more exact when necessary.

Commodity taxes can take many different forms. Some are general, in the sense that they are imposed on most commodities, even though in practice hardly any commodity tax is universal. Key examples are value added tax (VAT)[2] and general sales taxes levied on a wide range of goods with limited differentiation of rates. Other commodity taxes – commonly called excises or excise duties – are targeted at specific goods such as fuel and alcohol. They can take the form either of *ad valorem* taxes charged according to the value of a

---

[1] In common with general practice in economics, we will often use the word 'goods' to encompass all commodities, including services, although there will be places where we may need to distinguish between services and (physical) goods.

[2] Value added tax (VAT) – called Goods and Services Tax (GST) in some countries – takes the form of a sales tax initially levied on all sales, including those to other businesses as well as to final consumers; however, the ultimate effect of VAT is broadly, as we will see, to act as a tax on retail sales alone.

transaction or *specific* taxes, levied per unit, or based on a physical measure such as weight or volume.

One of the oldest forms of commodity taxes are trade tariffs. Historically these were a major source of public revenue. However, due to the liberalization of international trade over the years, the contribution of export and import tariffs to public revenue has diminished and is now very small in developed countries. They raise distinctive economic issues, which go beyond the scope of this Element, and we shall not consider tariffs in our discussion.

The economic and policy literature on taxation frequently makes use of a distinction between 'direct' taxes, such as the personal income tax, and 'indirect' taxes, such as VAT and other taxes on the sale of goods and services. Defining the precise meaning of 'indirect taxation', or setting the precise boundary between direct and indirect taxes so that all taxes fall in one or other category, is not wholly straightforward. The most common approach to systematic definition is one which distinguishes between taxes that are levied on identifiable persons, and which potentially can be differentiated according to their individual characteristics (such as total income, family size, etc.), and those which are levied on transactions (such as the sale of goods and services) and which impose an 'anonymous' tax burden, without reference to the characteristics or circumstances of the individuals affected.

Typically, with commodity taxes such as VAT, sellers of goods are required to account for the total value of their sales of taxable goods (possibly in various categories subject to different tax rates). A tax is calculated on this amount, and the seller must remit this tax to the government. The perception that this is an indirect tax reflects a view that the sellers would charge the tax as part of the price and hence the buyers are taxed in an indirect way. From this perspective the sellers are not the ultimate taxpayers, but merely operate as tax collectors for the government. To what extent sellers actually pass such taxes through to customers is a key economic question, to which we shall return.

In an important sense, most of our categories of taxation concern organizational form, rather than economic substance. A general sales tax could, in principle, be levied on all consumer spending, and if levied at a uniform rate on all goods and services (and if fully passed-on in prices) the total tax on a consumer's spending would be equivalent to applying the tax rate to the consumer's total spending. The same outcome could be achieved by levying an 'expenditure tax' on the individual's annual aggregate individual spending (computed as the difference between individual income and net saving). This (direct) expenditure tax was advocated, for example, by the Meade Report (1978) as a replacement for income tax, but such a tax has not been fully implemented anywhere. If the direct expenditure tax took account of no circumstances of the individual other than aggregate spending, its economic substance may be identical to the effect of a sales tax levied at a uniform rate on all categories of spending. However, the direct expenditure tax could instead be levied as a non-linear function of total spending, and also offers the possibility of taking account of various characteristics of the taxpayer that may be relevant in ensuring an equitable distribution of the overall tax burden between tax-payers. By contrast, the burden of a sales tax can only reflect taxpayer circum-stances very indirectly, by applying different rates of tax to goods that are more or less important in the spending of different types of household. Whether this is a serious drawback of indirect taxation is an issue that has been extensively discussed in the economics literature, but the contrast in principle between what can be achieved through direct and indirect taxation should be clear.

Another 'boundary' issue that is worth noting is the relationship between commodity taxes and various payments that governments may levy under the names of fees, tolls, charges, or duties to charge people for using certain goods or public services. Although the fees may be intended to charge people for the costs they impose on public services (such as publicly supplied energy, waste collection, transport, telecommunications services, etc.), they may be set at a level that raises net revenue for the government, in which case they are in effect commodity taxes without being formally defined as such. While we do not explicitly discuss public sector pricing here, we note the close similarities with the economic theory of commodity taxation. This is reflected in the term Ramsey–Boiteux pricing which integrates Ramsey's (1927) theory of optimal indirect taxation and Boiteux's (1956) optimal public sector pricing rule – the rule according to which prices ought to deviate from marginal costs as derived from second-best theory.

2 The Optimal Structure of Commodity Taxes

One of the enduring, seminal, papers in public economics lies at the heart of the theoretical literature on indirect taxation. A remarkable 1927 paper, written by Frank Ramsey, sought to give an answer to the question of what the pattern of tax rates across different goods and services should be, if the government's objective is to raise a given tax revenue at the least economic cost. The answer set out by Ramsey – loosely speaking, that tax rates should be set in inverse proportion to the elasticities of demand and supply – has been repeatedly revisited by public economists, leading to a series of papers which probe the precise conditions under which Ramsey's results hold.

The question Ramsey posed was beguilingly simple, albeit that the mathem-atics required to prove Ramsey's answer was far from straightforward. (The subsequent development of the theory of duality has greatly simplified the proof.) In Ramsey's problem, the government is constrained to use taxes on commodities to meet its given revenue requirement, and is taxing a population of identical individuals. Ramsey's conclusion – frequently interpreted as an 'inverse elasticity' rule – was explored in more detail by Corlett and Hague (1953), who demonstrated that the efficient pattern of tax rates involves higher taxes on goods that are more complementary with leisure – a result that has the appealing intuition that the indirect tax rates can be interpreted as compensating for the absence of a direct tax on leisure. Nevertheless, both Ramsey and Corlett and Hague derive their results in a context where the taxpaying population is homogeneous. In this context, it is unclear why indirect taxes are needed at all: a poll tax could raise the required revenue without incurring the costs of consumption distortions.

Subsequent literature has explored Ramsey's question in less-restrictive contexts: where individuals differ, so government objectives in revenue raising may need to take account of both efficiency and equity objectives; and where governments have a wider range of available tax instruments, including taxes on income as well as on spending. The most influential contribution has been Atkinson and Stiglitz (1976) who showed that when governments have the ability to levy sophisticated non-linear taxes on income, there are circumstances in which it will be optimal to levy taxes at a uniform rate on all goods and services – specifically where labour supply and commodity demands are separable. We shall single out for further discussion a number of aspects of the optimal structure of indirect taxes in the following sections. More issues are surveyed in Crawford et al. (2010), Boadway (2012), and Nygård and Revesz (2016).

2.1 A Closer Look at Corlett and Hague

While the inverse elasticity rule derived from Ramsey and the Corlett–Hague rule are both widely known, the literature does not often spell out their full implications and the relationship between them. We therefore believe that elaborating certain aspects of these tax rules is worthwhile.

The underlying model assumes that there is a single representative consumer or, equivalently, a population of identical consumers. There are two taxed market commodities and (untaxed) leisure. These goods are indexed 1, 2, and 0, respectively. For an agent, choosing leisure is obviously equivalent to choosing labour supply. Producer prices are fixed and equal to marginal (and average) cost. There is a fixed wage rate set equal to 1. Denote by t_i the tax on commodity i and let q_i be the consumer price. Let σ_{ij} denote the compensated elasticity of demand for good i with respect to the price of commodity j. It is trivial that taxing any market commodity will distort the trade-off between the taxed commodities and leisure, which is equivalent to distorting labour supply. Where the market commodities are taxed at different relative rates, there is also a distortion of the trade-off between them, which we shall refer to as distortion of the consumption bundle.

The optimal tax structure is the t_1, t_2 pair that maximizes utility, subject to a pre-set tax revenue requirement. In formal terms the objective is to maximize the indirect utility function $V(q_1, q_2)$ subject to $t_1 x_1(q_1, q_2) + t_2 x_2(q_1, q_2) = R_0$ for a given R_0, where $x_1(.)$ and $x_2(.)$ are demand functions. Optimum taxation can then be characterized by the following, known as the Corlett–Hague rule:

$$\frac{t_1/q_1}{t_2/q_2} = \frac{-\sigma_{11} - \sigma_{22} - \sigma_{10}}{-\sigma_{11} - \sigma_{22} - \sigma_{20}}.$$

We immediately see that commodity 1 or commodity 2 is taxed at a higher percentage rate according as $-\sigma_{10} > -\sigma_{20}$ $(\sigma_{20} > \sigma_{10})$ or $-\sigma_{10} < -\sigma_{20}$ $(\sigma_{10} > \sigma_{20})$. This means that a higher percentage tax rate is imposed on the commodity that is more complementary with leisure. Obviously, there is no differentiation in terms of relative tax rates if $\sigma_{10} = \sigma_{20}$. The interpretation is that the distortion of labour supply can be mitigated by taxing a commodity that is complementary with leisure. In the absence of a tax levied directly on leisure, this is an indirect way to tax it.

While only the value of $-\sigma_{10}$ relative to $-\sigma_{20}$ determines which tax rate should be higher, the size of $-\sigma_{11} - \sigma_{22}$ also influences the extent to which one would like to differentiate commodity taxes in case $\sigma_{10} \neq \sigma_{20}$. Letting commodity 1 be the more complementary with leisure such that $\frac{t_1/q_1}{t_2/q_2} > 1$, we note that a larger value of $-\sigma_{11} - \sigma_{22}$ implies a smaller percentage increase of the numerator than of the denominator. The effect is to diminish the ratio and move it closer to 1. Accordingly, there is less differentiation. This effect reflects that we should also take into account the distortion of the consumption bundle in addition to the labour supply distortion. This becomes more transparent when noting that $-\sigma_{11} = \sigma_{12} + \sigma_{10}$ and $-\sigma_{22} = \sigma_{21} + \sigma_{20}$, so that for given values of σ_{10} and σ_{20} larger values of $-\sigma_{11}$ and $-\sigma_{22}$ reflect a larger degree of substitution between the taxed commodities. Substituting for $-\sigma_{11}$ and $-\sigma_{22}$, we can write the Corlett–Hague rule as $\frac{t_1/q_1}{t_2/q_2} = \frac{\sigma_{12} + \sigma_{21} + \sigma_{20}}{\sigma_{12} + \sigma_{21} + \sigma_{10}}$. This may be a more instructive way to express the condition. Larger values of σ_{12} and σ_{21} imply that further differentiation of prices will induce stronger substitution between taxed commodities which exacerbates the distortion of the consumption bundle. This is a case for a more modest differentiation of taxes and prices. For sufficiently large values of σ_{12} and σ_{21}, the ratio will approach 1 and the tax differentiation will vanish. We can conclude that the optimal tax rule expresses a trade-off between the desire to diminish the labour supply distortion and the desire to avoid a large distortion of the consumption bundle.

We note that when $\sigma_{10} = \sigma_{20} = 0$, uniform percentage taxation is always optimal. Since there is no substitution between taxed commodities and leisure, the only potential inefficiency is a distortion of the consumption bundle which can always be avoided by refraining from differentiating tax rates.

Now consider the case where there is no substitution between taxed commodities: $\sigma_{12} = \sigma_{21} = 0$. Hence $\sigma_{11} + \sigma_{10} = \sigma_{22} + \sigma_{20} = 0$, and $\frac{t_1/q_1}{t_2/q_2} = \frac{-\sigma_{22}}{-\sigma_{11}}$, which alternatively can be written as $\frac{t_1}{q_1} = \frac{a}{-\sigma_{11}}$ and $\frac{t_2}{q_2} = \frac{a}{-\sigma_{22}}$ for some $a > 0$ determined by the tax revenue requirement. This tax rule is the familiar 'inverse elasticity rule', frequently highlighted in basic presentations of optimal commodity taxes, under which the tax rate is proportional to the inverse of the own price elasticity. We should note that since $-\sigma_{11} = \sigma_{10}$ and $-\sigma_{22} = \sigma_{20}$, the inverse own price elasticity rule is equivalent to $\frac{t_1/q_1}{t_2/q_2} = \frac{-\sigma_{20}}{-\sigma_{10}}$ or as $\frac{t_1}{q_1} = \frac{a}{\sigma_{10}}$ and $\frac{t_2}{q_2} = \frac{a}{\sigma_{20}}$. These inverse *cross price* elasticity rules highlight the links to the labour market and may be more illuminating than the standard formulations.

We see that, as in the aforementioned general case, which tax rate is set at a higher value depends on the relative complementarity of commodity demand with leisure. What is different in this case is that since there is no substitution between taxed commodities, no effect on the distortion of the consumption bundle appears in the optimal tax rule. A low absolute value of the own price elasticity now simply reflects weak substitutability with leisure and warrants a relatively high tax rate.

It is important to note that the estimates of σ_{11} and σ_{22} required for implementing the taxes prescribed by the Corlett–Hague rule are those describing demand responses in a setting where commodity demand and labour supply are chosen simultaneously. It is not obvious how low or high estimates of own price elasticities under a fixed total consumption expenditure translate to the commodity demand–labour supply model.

Dixit (1975) provides a generalization to more than two taxed commodities. A different extension would be to consider more untaxed goods. There may be goods that are administratively difficult to tax. An even more compelling case is goods consumed abroad by tourists from the home country under consideration (sight-seeing, foreign hotel accommodation, etc.). Since this consumption takes place outside the jurisdiction of the government of the home country, taxation by the home country is obviously impossible. We discuss further international aspects of taxation in Section 6.

Let us now add a further untaxable good, denoted good 3, to our model. We can then easily derive a Corlett–Hague rule for this case:

$$\frac{t_1/q_1}{t_2/q_2} = \frac{-\sigma_{11} - \sigma_{22} - \sigma_{10} - \sigma_{13}}{-\sigma_{11} - \sigma_{22} - \sigma_{20} - \sigma_{23}}.$$

Now we note that also the cross effect to the additional untaxed good matters. For example, suppose that good 1 is domestic tourism and good 3 is the fairly close substitute tourism taking place abroad. Then σ_{13} is positive and conceivably fairly large, implying that good 1 (tourism at home) should be taxed more leniently than otherwise. The example should just be considered as an illustration. A full analysis of the taxation of tourism should clearly also allow for taxation of goods typically purchased by foreign tourists in the home country.

We now return to the setting with a single untaxed good, interpreted as leisure. Taking a general income tax as point of departure, Meade (1955) argued that tax rates on various goods should depend on how demands for the goods are related to leisure (or labour). Meade concluded that welfare would be enhanced by a marginal change in the tax system, which raises the price of those things that are jointly demanded with leisure, and lowers the price of work-related things. One may think respectively of leisure goods (e.g. sports equipment or concert tickets) and goods consumed while working (e.g. childcare or clothes worn at work). However, it is not trivial which time uses one should consider as work or leisure, respectively. Often the distinction is made between work for pay in the market and leisure, but then one observes that many 'leisure activities' are similar to activities that other people carry out as paid work (house maintenance, gardening, cleaning, etc.). Other 'leisure activities' require unpleasant use of time (pure travel time, time at the dentist's, household chores, etc.), hardly experienced as significantly different from time doing market work. Even if it is a pleasure, using leisure goods takes time. Fishing rods, skis, and books are not of value unless time is made available to use them. The time used for consuming a leisure good must then compete with time used for market work, for consuming other leisure goods, or for pure leisure (rest) without consuming particular goods (listening to the birds or enjoying the sunset). A series of papers have addressed these various aspects of time use in the context of indirect taxation.

Sandmo (1990) and Kleven et al. (2000) drew attention to the fact that several commodities can either be purchased in the market or produced by own efforts in the household and argued that optimal taxation should favour market-produced services which are close substitutes for home-produced services.

Christiansen (1984) introduced the Becker–Lancaster approach to model the enjoyment of leisure, or recreation, as an activity using time and market goods as inputs. (Becker, 1965; Lancaster, 1966). By taxing leisure goods purchased in the market, recreation is made less attractive compared to work, but the paper highlights a further effect: when taxed, leisure goods may be substituted by leisure time in the 'production' of recreation and, with strong substitutability, less time may actually be devoted to work. It follows that it is not necessarily appropriate to recommend taxation of leisure goods, even if one is willing to make the plausible assumption that they are technical complements with leisure within a Becker–Lancaster framework. Recreation may simply be made more time-intensive and less commodity-intensive. To give an extreme example, one might substitute a long, cheap, cottage holiday for a short, service-intensive, luxury cruise.

Later papers by Gahvari and Yang (1993) and Kleven (2004) took a similar approach in that they considered taxation of market goods used to transform time into utility in the spirit of Becker and Lancaster. These papers carry out a more extensive analysis with an arbitrary number of activities, but rule out substitution between the factors own time and market goods in each activity. The optimal tax rule is a simple inverse factor share rule: the tax rate on any given market good is inversely proportional to its factor share. In a special case, the consumer allocates his entire time endowment to activities, all of which require an input of time and of market goods with fixed input coefficients. By taxing the input of market goods, one can indirectly tax the entire time endowment of the consumer to achieve the first best. Another case is the one where part of the time endowment is allocated to pure, untaxed leisure alongside the allocation of time to activities also requiring material input. The inverse factor share rule is then modified by a Corlett–Hague factor, reducing to an inverse elasticity factor in the absence of cross-price effects as in the simple Ramsey model.

Boadway and Gahvari (2006) brought together many of the aspects of time use mentioned previously. They distinguish between uses of time generating disutility (labour or household work, etc.) and uses of time generating utility either directly as leisure in isolation (pure leisure or rest) or in combination with goods purchased in the market (museum tickets, music, etc.). Consumption of a good requires a fixed amount of time that is either unpleasant and is a perfect labour substitute or is enjoyable and is a perfect substitute for pure leisure.[3] Leaving details and caveats aside, we can roughly summarize the overall insights from the paper as follows: For goods requiring leisure-equivalent time, the optimal tax rules are the standard ones. Goods for which the time spent consuming them is unpleasant and labour-equivalent, should *ceteris paribus* be taxed at a higher rate than those for which the time use is pleasant.

---

[3] In this respect, the paper is inspired by Gahvari (2007).

The more time-intensive these market goods are in consumption, the greater the need for the tax rates to be higher.

The Corlet–Hague and inverse elasticity rule are derived under the strict assumption that there is a homogenous population. To extend the analysis to models with a heterogeneous population and distributional concerns, we consider a simple setting with two (types of) agents, type 1 and type 2, where the latter is the richer, for instance, due to a higher wage rate. We assume that the policy instruments are two commodity taxes and a lump sum transfer, denoted by a. We denote prices by q_1 and q_2. The social welfare function is the sum of (indirect) utilities: $V^1(q_1, q_2, a) + V^2(q_1, q_2, a)$, and the tax revenue requirement is

$t_1\left(x_1^1 + x_1^2\right) + t_2\left(x_2^1 + x_2^2\right) - 2a = R_0$, where superscripts denote types of agent. To maximize welfare, we formulate the Lagrange function:

$$V^1(q_1, q_2, a) + V^2(q_1, q_2, a) + \mu\left(t_1\left(x_1^1 + x_1^2\right) + t_2\left(x_2^1 + x_2^2\right) - 2a - R_0\right).$$

To summarize the trade-offs that characterize the tax optimum, we can derive the following condition which expresses the effects of shifting the tax burden from commodity 2 to commodity 1: $\left[\frac{t_1}{q_1}(\sigma_{11} + \sigma_{22} + \sigma_{20})\right.$ $\left. - \frac{t_2}{q_2}(\sigma_{22} + \sigma_{11} + \sigma_{10})\right] + (\Lambda^1 - \Lambda^2)\left(\frac{x_2^1}{X_2} - \frac{x_1^1}{X_1}\right) + (m^1 - m^2)\left(\frac{x_2^1}{X_2} - \frac{x_1^1}{X_1}\right) = 0$, where $m^i = t_1\frac{\partial x_1^i}{\partial y^i} + t_2\frac{\partial x_2^i}{\partial y^i}$, to which we shall return later. $\Lambda^i = \frac{\lambda^i}{\mu}$ we interpret as the welfare weight assigned to marginal income accruing to agent i.

The Appendix shows how the first order conditions are derived.

This optimal tax condition comprises three main terms. The first term in brackets consists of the Corlett–Hague terms capturing the labour supply and consumption bundle distortions discussed previously. We note that in the special case of identical agents, the condition reduces to the pure Corlett–Hague rule. The second term captures the distributional effects. Where it is desirable to redistribute income from the richer type 2 to the poorer type 1 (i.e. $\Lambda^1 > \Lambda^2$), shifting taxes from commodity 2 to commodity 1 has a beneficial welfare effect where the poorer agent's consumption share is smaller for commodity 1 than for commodity 2. The reason is that for a marginal tax increase that is fully passed on to the consumer price, the consumption share of an agent reflects the consumer's share of the tax burden.[4] Finally, if we consider the third term, this can be interpreted as an efficiency effect of redistribution. The reason is that the commodity taxes are wedges between the consumers' marginal commodity valuation and the marginal cost. It follows

---

[4] The burden of a price increase measured as loss of real income is $-\frac{\partial V^i/\partial q_k}{\partial V^i/\partial y^i} = x_k^i$, where x_k^i is agent i's consumption of commodity k. The fraction of the burden is x_k^i/X_k, where $X_k = \sum_i x_k^i$.

that greater consumption of a taxed commodity is efficiency enhancing, and this effect will be greater the higher the tax and the larger the demand response. Taken together, these determine the change in tax revenue, which in this case measures the efficiency gain. We can interpret m^i as agent i's marginal propensity to pay tax, that is, the additional tax revenue generated by giving an extra unit of income to agent i. When there is a redistribution of income from agent 2 to agent 1 determined by the consumption shares, as shown, the effect on tax revenue depends on the difference between the respective marginal propensities of the two agents to pay taxes. Obviously, the term vanishes in the case of equal marginal propensities.

2.2 Commodity Taxes and Product Innovation

Even though most normative theories of commodity taxation confine attention to quantities consumed of a fixed range of goods of given quality, taxes can also affect quality and product diversity. Kay and Keen (1983) discuss how the level and form of commodity taxation affect these welfare-relevant properties of consumption goods. Subject to certain fairly plausible assumptions, they show that firms' choice of quality is unaffected by a specific commodity tax whereas an *ad valorem* tax causes a downward distortion of quality. The intuition is that better quality requires a higher price and is therefore taxed more per unit. A similar result in a monopolistic competition model is that product variety is a decreasing function of the *ad valorem* tax rate but is independent of the specific tax. The factor underlying this result is that since an *ad valorem* tax involves a relatively low retail price, it also implies a relatively low degree of product diversity. In brief, the *ad valorem* component of commodity taxation can be perceived as a tax on quality and product variety. While detrimental to product quality, the *ad valorem* tax can therefore be used as a corrective device to guide the amount of product diversity towards the socially optimal level.

In practice, differential commodity taxation requires that commodities be divided into discrete categories defined by certain characteristics of the goods. One must draw lines between the categories, for example, raw food (for humans), take-away meals, fast food, restaurant meals, pet-food, etc., not to mention a conceivable distinction between healthy and unhealthy food. Such line-drawing raises a number of issues regarding desirable differentiation, administrative costs, and enforcement problems. Trading off the various concerns, what is the optimal partition and associated tax differentiation? An important concern is inefficiencies due to tax-driven innovations, meaning that products are (re)designed to move them just across the line to the lower-taxed category, which gives rise to socially inefficient product differentiation in pursuit of tax savings. The socially

harmful innovations must be traded off against an imperfect pattern of differentiation from a conventional optimal tax perspective. The literature has discussed
the optimal differentiation when differentiation is administratively costly and the
special case where, for that reason, the number of tax categories is constrained.

The literature on the various aspects of grouping of commodities includes
Belan et al. (2008), Gilitzer et al. (2017), Gordon (1989), and Wilson (1989).

2.3 Optimal Commodity Taxes with Income Taxation

It is often claimed that a consumption tax is regressive. The key argument seems to
be the presumption that people with higher income save a larger fraction of income
than those with lower income. Since a consumption tax taxes only consumption
and not savings, it will tax a lower share of higher incomes. However, this
reasoning neglects the taxation of future consumption. To consider the intertemporal choice in a two-period setting, denote by y_1, c_1 and y_2, c_2, respectively, the
gross income and consumption in the first period and in the second period. Let i
denote the interest rate used for discounting. To allow for taxes, let t be the tax rate
on income and let τ be the tax rate on consumption. The intertemporal budget
constraint is then $(1 - t)y_1 + (1 - t)\frac{1}{1+i}y_2 = (1 + \tau)c_1 + (1 + \tau)\frac{1}{1+i}c_2$, when
the pre-tax price of consumption is normalized to 1. Then consider tax incre-
ments dt and $d\tau$. By invoking the envelope theorem, we can neglect the induced
changes in consumption when considering the utility impact of small tax
changes. The respective changes in the tax burden are then $\left(y_1 + \frac{1}{1+i}y_2\right)dt$
and $\left(c_1 + \frac{1}{1+i}c_2\right)d\tau = \frac{1-t}{1+\tau}\left(y_1 + \frac{1}{1+i}y_2\right)d\tau$. We see that in either case the additional tax burden is proportional to the discounted income. The tax as a share of
(discounted) aggregate income is independent of income level. We may also
note that an increase in the consumption tax rate will erode the real value of
initial wealth, hitting the rich rather than the poor.

Whatever the distributional impact of commodity taxes, there is considerable
scope to offset this through adjustments to other taxes where these are also levied,
in particular through income tax. Indeed, where available, direct taxes and transfers may outperform commodity taxes as redistributive tools. We may note that
already a uniform lump-sum transfer will favour low income households more
than do commodity subsidies under the weak assumption that the subsidized
consumption increases with income. Where the aim is to favour a particular
group (e.g. families with children), an earmarked transfer, such as a child benefit,
is more accurately targeted than a commodity tax reduction on certain goods,
which would confer a benefit indiscriminately to all consumers.

As an income tax will always distort labour supply, the conceivable mitigat-
ing role of commodity taxes, considered previously, is still of relevance.

Whether there should be a separate role for commodity taxes in redistributing income is less clear. The latter concern is obviously more important if stronger restrictions are imposed on the income tax, limiting the scope for tailoring the tax to distributional preferences.

To consider the weakest possible case for commodity taxes, we can abstract from all restrictions but those that are strictly unavoidable. In the Mirrlees tradition of tax theory, the only fundamental restriction is assumed to be the informational constraint that the government does not know the identity of, respectively, high-skilled and low-skilled agents. This can be translated into a self-selection constraint requiring that the tax intended for a type of agent is set such that it will not be in the self-interest of other types to qualify for this tax. If finding it in their interest, other types might acquire the same tax liability by choosing the same taxable income through adjustment of labour supply. The other types would then be said to mimic.

The simplest framework for discussing income and commodity taxation from the aforementioned perspective is to consider a model where there is a high-skilled agent facing a high exogenous wage rate and a low-skilled agent with a low wage rate, each choosing how much labour to supply and consequently how much income to earn.[5] We assume that an inequality-averse government wants to impose a higher tax on the high-skilled type for distributional reasons. The extent to which the tax liability can be differentiated will then be constrained by the self-selection constraint, which requires that the high-skilled type is no better off mimicking. For a binding constraint, the high-skilled type must be equally well off choosing the income and associated tax intended for him as he would be choosing the income intended for the low-skilled type.[6] As is well known, the behaviour of the low-skilled person is distorted. There is a downward distortion of labour supply.

Keeping a tax revenue requirement fixed, the only way to enhance welfare in this economy is to relax the self-selection constraint. The crucial question is whether this can be achieved by resorting to commodity taxes. We can then explore the effects of levying a tax on a commodity. To make the tax reform revenue neutral, we also lower the respective income taxes of the high-skilled and the low-skilled agent, keeping the respective tax burdens unchanged. If the high-skilled agent were to mimic the low-skilled one, he would then get the same income tax relief as the latter, but his commodity tax burden need not be the same. If he consumes more of the good in question, the high-skilled mimicker would

---

[5] This model is known as the two-type Mirrlees model; see Stern (1982) and Stiglitz (1982).

[6] As is common, we make the simplifying assumption that there is no mimicking in the case of indifference rather than working with the technically awkward case that one is infinitesimally close to indifference.

incur a larger burden. It follows that since only the smaller burden of the low-skilled type is compensated by the income tax relief, the mimicker is under-compensated and is made worse off. This means that mimicking becomes unattractive. The self-selection constraint has been relaxed. A new allocation becomes available that could make either agent better off. In other words, the commodity tax would render a Pareto improvement possible. To see the circumstance in which this would happen, we note that the only difference between the mimicker and the low-skilled agent is that the former enjoys more leisure. Having a larger wage rate, he can earn the same income in less time. The implication is that it is beneficial to tax a commodity which is complementary with leisure in the sense that more is consumed if the consumer has more leisure. If the converse is true, so that more is consumed if the consumer has less leisure (and works more), welfare could be enhanced by subsidizing the good. It follows that if we have the case in between that demand for the good in question is independent of leisure (and labour), there is nothing to gain by taxing or subsidizing the good. One can show that demand being independent of leisure is equivalent to the utility function exhibiting (at least) weak separability between market goods and leisure. Then there is no case for (positive or negative) commodity tax. This is the famous Atkinson–Stiglitz theorem.

Once there is a case for introducing a commodity tax, two concerns will govern its optimal value. One is its ability to relax the self-selection constraint, equivalent to alleviation of the labour supply distortion. The other is the distortion of the consumption bundle that it incurs. We note that the trade-off is similar in nature to the trade-off discussed in the Corlett–Hague model. With several potential taxes, the effects of all the taxes on the self-selection constraint will matter, and both own effects and cross effects will determine the extent to which the consumption bundle is distorted. With several commodity taxes, it is less clear that there will be a commodity subsidy on a good that is negatively associated with leisure. It may only be taxed at a low rate relative to other goods.

A number of papers have addressed the mixed taxation of commodities and income discussed previously. Christiansen (1984) asked the question which commodity taxes should supplement the income tax. Stiglitz (1982) discussed the general case where non-linear taxes can be imposed both on income and commodities. Non-linear taxation of each consumer's consumption of a commodity requires information about the amount consumed by each person. This information is available only in a few cases, typically where the consumer subscribes to delivery through some energy or telecommunications network. In practice, almost all commodity taxes are imposed on anonymous transactions and have to be linear. Edwards et al. (1994) characterize optimal mixed income and linear commodity taxation in a two-type Mirrless model. In this setting, they emphasize the importance of considering effective tax rates which reflect tax liability due to both income and commodity taxes. Labour wedges include, besides the income tax, an additional term due to commodity taxes. They highlight that any Pareto-efficient differentiated commodity tax structure has the feature that a mimicking high-ability person would pay strictly more commodity tax than does the low-ability individual. This is the key to understanding the ability of commodity taxes to offset some of the distortions created by the income tax by weakening the self-selection constraint, which is the very source of the distortions. Jacobs and Boadway (2014) provide a full characterization of optimal linear commodity taxation under optimal non-linear income taxation with a continuum of agents. They emphasize that the results are very much in the nature of the Corlett–Hague insight. Commodity tax differentiation is desirable only if it prompts labour supply.

We see that with a redistributive income tax in place, a role for commodity taxes may be to alleviate the inefficiencies that arise. While we may conceive of the effects as pure efficiency gains in terms of Pareto improvements, we may also see them as ways to diminish the social cost of redistribution. In this sense, commodity taxes may have a supportive role for other policy instruments that are primary tools for achieving redistribution.

In practice, one may wonder how far one should go in differentiating commodity taxes in order to stimulate labour supply. It may be that singling out for subsidization or public provision a few strong complements with labour (e.g. child-care) is sufficient and administratively tractable. For further discussion of this issue, see Crawford et al. (2010) and Bastani et al. (2015).

The papers mentioned here all make the standard assumption that agents have identical preferences. Saez (2002) analyses the implications of preference heterogeneity and shows that goods for which high-income earners have a higher taste should be taxed more.

The result that optimal taxation may rely solely on taxation of income with commodity taxes being redundant and the finding that, if differentiated, commodity taxes are used for efficiency reasons to alleviate income tax distortions of labour supply, are based on the assumption that income is a satisfactory indicator of standard of living. Where taxable income is biased by evasion or failure to include certain types of income, or there are other untaxed sources of economic welfare, the composition of the consumption bundle may convey additional information on the standard of living. Then there may be a case for deploying differentiated commodity taxes alongside a progressive income tax to achieve a further direct impact on distribution,[7] not only to improve the efficiency of the income tax.

---

[7] In addition, a further dimension of redistribution that may be affected by the level and pattern of commodity taxes is the within-household distribution as addressed by Bargain and Donni (2014)

3 Commodity Tax Incidence

In this section, we turn to questions of incidence, in other words, the extent to which a tax levied on sales is passed on to consumers.

The most well-known incidence model to any student of economics is certainly the partial equilibrium model of a competitive market. A tax will disturb the market equilibrium and prices must adjust to restore equilibrium. Imposing a specific tax on a commodity will lower the producer price and increase the consumer price. The consumer price will increase by no more than the tax, and likewise the producer price will fall by an amount at most equal to the tax. How the respective prices respond depends on the slopes of the demand and supply curves. The side of the market with the steeper curve will experience the larger price change. An important observation is that only the slopes of supply and demand schedules matter, unlike in the case of imperfect competition to which we turn our attention now.

In small open economies, it is common to assume that the agents face fixed world market prices, which is equivalent to completely elastic supply. While this is in numerous cases a plausible assumption, there are important exceptions. A major reason is international price discrimination. Large international enterprises exerting market power may respond to market conditions and taxes even in small open economies. This is a circumstance that governments in small open economies may like to take into account when setting taxes. It will be in the interest of an importing country to shift taxes to foreign suppliers or limit their incentive to increase prices.

The simplest imperfect competition case is a market with a monopoly. A tax will be a cost item for the monopolist reducing the profit per unit. The question is how a tax will affect the price setting of the monopolist. In the optimum, the monopolist will trade off two effects. Charging the consumer a larger price will enable the monopolist to earn a larger profit on each unit, but the number of units sold will diminish. The immediate effect of a specific tax (for a constant consumer price) is to lower the profit per unit. This will diminish the loss a monopolist incurs by selling fewer units, making him more willing to raise the consumer price and accept smaller sales. A well-known special case is that when supply and demand curves are linear and the marginal production cost is constant, half of the tax will show up as an increase in the consumer price and the other half as a reduction in the producer price (consumer price minus the unit tax). Only half of the tax is passed through, or shifted, to the consumer price. In general, the pass-through may be larger or smaller and the consumer price increase may even exceed the tax increase (i.e. there is over-shifting).

As is well known, under perfect competition, *ad valorem* and specific taxes are equivalent. The reason is obviously that for a price taker it makes no difference whether a tax is related to an, for her or him, exogenous price or not. This is different in the monopoly case where switching to an *ad valorem* tax (specific tax) will induce the monopolist to reduce (increase) the price he charges.

Like a specific tax, an *ad valorem* tax will diminish the profit per unit and hence reduce the loss incurred by selling a smaller quantity, but now a further effect will arise. When charging a larger consumer price, part of the increase is taxed away by an *ad valorem* tax, and the monopolist is left with a smaller rise in profits per unit. There is a weaker case for raising the consumer price, and it will be increased less than in the specific tax regime.

To take a formal approach, we make use of the following notation. Denote by c the marginal cost of production, x, and denote by t and τ, respectively, a specific tax rate and an *ad valorem* tax rate, defined as a fraction of the pre-tax price. We let p and q be the producer price and the consumer price, respectively. We denote by x' the demand response (in absolute value) to a one-unit price increase and by $\varepsilon = qx'/x$ the price elasticity in absolute value. We shall make use of the fact that there is over- (under)-shifting if the before-tax price increases (decreases). The first order conditions for profit maximization imply that:

(a) with specific taxation

$$q = (c + t)\frac{\varepsilon}{\varepsilon - 1}$$

and the price net-of-tax is

$$p = q - t = (c + t)\frac{\varepsilon}{\varepsilon - 1} - t = c\frac{\varepsilon}{\varepsilon - 1} + \frac{1}{\varepsilon - 1}t.$$

Assuming a constant elasticity,

$$\frac{dp}{dt} = \frac{1}{\varepsilon - 1} > 0.$$

There is over-shifting. We also note that the closer ε is to 1, in other words, the less elastic is demand, the greater is dp/dt and the extent of over-shifting.

(b) with *ad valorem* taxation

$$q = c\frac{\varepsilon}{\varepsilon - 1}(1 + \tau)$$

$$p = q - \frac{\tau}{1 + \tau}q = \frac{q}{1 + \tau} = c\frac{\varepsilon}{\varepsilon - 1}.$$

Assuming a constant elasticity,

$$\frac{dp}{d\tau} = 0.$$

There is neither over-shifting nor under-shifting. In either case, other results may arise if the elasticity changes in response to a change in q.

A number of papers have discussed over-shifting. Weyl and Fabinger (2013) and Pless and Benthem (2019) make precise in what sense convexity of the demand function is required to yield over-shifting in the monopoly case. Since over-shifting is ruled out under perfect competition, its appearance is evidence of market power, as studied, also empirically, by Pless and Benthem (2019) using data from the solar energy market in California.

The tax shifting effect on prices is often presented as a question of who pays the tax: the consumer or the producer. In the competitive case this makes good sense, but in general this perspective may be a bit misleading. The changes in the consumer price and the producer price, respectively, do not necessarily reflect, in an adequate way, how the tax burden is divided between consumers and producers, defined as owners of enterprises. For instance, saying that the consumer share of the tax burden is 102 per cent (and implicitly the producer's share –2 per cent) is likely to be confusing.

Price changes will involve real income changes for producers and consumers that one can derive, respectively, from utility functions and profit functions. We consider a small tax increment. Where both consumers and producers are price takers, the consumers' income loss is xdq, while the producers' income loss is $-xdp$. The sum is $x(dq-dp) = xdt$, and it is trivial that dq and $-dp$ are the respective shares of the tax burden. If instead the producer is a monopolist, the matter is more complex. We can write the profit function as $\pi = (q - t)x(q) - c\big(x(q)\big)$, where $x(.)$ and $c(.)$ denote, respectively, the demand function and the cost function. The producer maximizes profits with respect to the price q, and it follows from the envelope theorem that $-d\pi = xdt$, while the consumers' real income loss is $xdq = (q - c - t)(-dx/dq)dq$ due to the monopolist's optimality condition.[8] Defining the producer price by $p = q - t$, as noted, we have that $-dp = dt - dq$ but $-xdp = x(dt - dq)$, which is less than xdt for any $dq > 0$. In the monopoly case $-xdp$ does not reflect the burden on the producer. Where over-shifting occurs (i.e. $dq > dt$), it might be tempting to think that the tax increase would benefit the producer. When this does not happen, it is because of the standard

---

[8] The government's revenue gain is $xdq + t(dx/dq)dq$, and summing the public and private effects, the social loss is $(q - c)(-dx/dq)dq$. We get the excess burden, part of which is borne by the consumers.

envelope property that an optimizing monopolist can only derive second-order and negligible benefits from increasing the price, even beyond the tax increase. The reason is that the partial gain from the price increase is offset by the reduction in quantity that is indeed a consequence of charging a higher price. However, one should note that it makes a difference if a monopoly is replaced by oligopoly. The reason is that, unlike monopolists in full control of the price, oligopolists do not maximize industry profits. It will be in their common interest that a smaller output is supplied, for instance as a response to a tax.

Commodity taxes in oligopoly and monopsonistic markets are discussed in Stern (1987). Building on Seade (1985) and Dixit and Stern (1982), Stern developed a conjectural model nesting a range of market forms including generalized-Cournot and monopolistic competition. In generalized-Cournot, the profit maximizing behaviour of each firm is based on the conjecture that if its own output goes up by 1 per cent, that of the rest of the market goes up by α per cent, where in most cases $0 \leq \alpha \leq 1$. In generalized-Cournot, the number of firms in the market is fixed. Monopolistic competition is characterized by free entry and zero profits. It is shown that, as in the monopoly case, the effect on price of a unit tax increase can be greater or smaller than 1. The former case materializes if the elasticity of the price elasticity is sufficiently small in absolute value. An increase in a unit tax increases the number of firms in monopolistic competition if and only if it would increase profits in generalized-Cournot given the number of firms. The effect on price under generalized-Cournot is lower than in monopolistic competition if and only if a tax decreases profits in generalized-Cournot. Then there will be fewer firms in monopolistic competition.

Delipalla and Keen (1992) find that both in the generalized-Cournot and free-entry oligopoly models *ad valorem* taxes are less likely to be over-shifted than specific taxes and increasing *ad valorem* taxes is less likely to raise profits than is increasing specific taxation. The latter result is obviously related to the difference in price effects. A lower price is bad for profits.[9] A closely related result is that in either regime a shift from specific to *ad valorem* taxation leads to a strict reduction in the consumer price. There is a strict reduction in profits in the generalized-Cournot regime, and a strict reduction in the number of active firms in the free entry oligopoly case.

We observe that several oligopoly results are generalizations of the findings in the monopoly case. A trivial difference is of course that also considering the free entry case allows us to take into account the number of firms. A more

---

[9] This is different from the monopoly case where the producer fully controls the price, and there is no first order gain of changing the price where optimality is pursued.

interesting difference is that in the oligopoly case there is a fiscal externality since a change in a firm's supply will affect the price also facing other firms, making it possible that a tax-induced decline in supply and ensuing price increase can raise industry profits. In a non-cooperative equilibrium, a tax will serve as an incentive for each agent to opt for a lower output that will drive up the price but at a cost in terms of a tax burden. Profits will only rise where the induced price increase outweighs the tax burden. Weyl and Fabinger (2013) presents a very general approach that nests a number of models including perfect competition and a variety of models of symmetric as well as asymmetric imperfect competition. The key unifying concept in their analysis is a so-called conduct parameter which, denoted by θ, is defined in our notation as $\theta = [(q - c - t)/q]\varepsilon$, the elasticity-adjusted Lerner index in the symmetric case. The analysis shows how the θ set by firms in the various cases as well as the properties of the parameter determine the tax incidence. As is intuitive, the less competitive conduct is (the larger is θ), the more of taxation is borne by firms relative to consumers.

The conventional wisdom that the tax incidence is independent of which agents remit the tax is challenged when supply and demand do not only depend on (tax-inclusive and tax-exclusive) prices, but taxes play a separate role, for instance, because taxes are evaded. Kopczuk et al. (2016) show that shifting the tax remittance to the sector with less tax-elastic evasion results in higher pass-through of the tax.

Before closing the theoretical discussion of tax incidence, a caveat may be in order. One should bear in mind that the partial market equilibrium analysis commonly used to discuss tax incidence may be too limited because there may be other repercussions, for instance, in terms of lower wages, due to either general equilibrium effects or bargaining. Empirical evidence on the extent to which VAT and other indirect taxes are passed through to consumer prices has been most widely researched at the sub-national level. The differences in the rates of retail sales taxes set by local governments in the United States provide a promising focus for empirical research on incidence. For example, Besley and Rosen (1999) used data on the prices of twelve specific commodities in 155 US cities to assess the extent to which differences in the sales tax rates are reflected in prices, controlling for cost differences between cities. They found that shifting patterns vary widely between commodities, with some exhibiting full shifting of taxes onto prices (which would be consistent with a competitive market and a horizontal long-run supply curve), while more than half the commodities showed varying amounts of over-shifting (which would be consistent with some form of imperfect competition). Miravete et al. (2018) address the relationship between an excise tax on alcohol and tax revenue – the Laffer curve – under oligopolistic pricing. The paper models and estimates empirically both spirit demand and distillers' pricing behaviour in Pennsylvania, allowing for differentiated products and heterogeneous preferences within the population. Distillers respond to tax increases by lowering the pre-tax price they charge. The response of non-competitive firms significantly alters and flattens the Laffer curve compared with that under perfect competition.

Within Europe, VAT rates are set at the national level, and cultural and marketing differences between countries make it more difficult to use variation across jurisdictions to investigate incidence. Much of the research evidence from Europe exploits VAT changes on some particular commodities, especially labour-intensive services, facilitated by an EU decision to permit member states to make tax changes in this area, with difference-in-difference methods typically used to compare the effects with similar sectors unaffected by any tax change. In France, Carbonnier (2007), for example, found that consumers experienced 57 per cent of the benefit of a reduction in the VAT rate on car sales in 1987, and 77 per cent of a VAT cut on housing repair services in 1999, while Benzarti and Carloni (2019) found that very little of a French VAT cut on restaurant meals in 2009 was passed through in prices. In Finland, Kosonen (2015) found that only about 50 per cent of a reduction in the VAT rate on hairdresser services was passed through to consumers. By contrast Harju et al. (2018) found that restaurant price responses to VAT reductions in Finland (in 2010) and Sweden (in 2012), varied between full and no pass-through, with chain restaurants more likely than independent restaurants to pass through the tax change. Gaarder (2018) studied a halving of the VAT rate on food items in Norway in 2001, using a regression discontinuity approach, and concluded that the effect was completely shifted to consumer prices. One striking finding from Benzarti et al. (2020), a Europe-wide study of VAT reforms from 1996 to 2015, was that consumer prices do not respond symmetrically to increases and decreases in the VAT: the effect of a VAT increase was found to be three to four times larger than an equivalent VAT reduction.

4 Economic Aspects of the VAT

Levying a tax on all sales of goods and services would tax both sales of intermediate goods and services between enterprises, as well as sales to final consumers. If the chain of production involves a number of intermediate transactions, all of which are subject to taxation, then the total tax on sales to final consumers could include a considerable amount of tax accumulated from earlier transactions. The overall burden of tax on a particular commodity sold to a final consumer would depend on the number of intermediate transactions, and their value, giving rise to a significant incentive for vertical integration to minimize the number of taxed intermediate transactions. In modern economies such 'cascade taxes' are rare.

An important paper by Diamond and Mirrlees (1971) has demonstrated that, under certain conditions, economic efficiency requires that revenue-raising taxes should be imposed on sales to final consumers only, while intermediate transactions should be unburdened by taxation. In principle there are two broad routes to this outcome.

One is to limit the scope of sales taxation to sales made to final consumers only, by levying a retail sales tax (RST). The vendor is required to determine whether each sale is an intermediate transaction to another enterprise, or a sale to a final consumer, and to charge tax only in the latter case. In some cases this 'end user' distinction may be difficult to determine, leaving scope for sales tax evasion through mis-classification of transactions. In practice, the RST systems operated by many US states levy tax on a significant number of intermediate goods transactions, leading to some cascading of the tax burden.

An alternative approach, which in general should lead to an identical tax burden on sales to final consumers, is to levy a value added tax (VAT), under which all sales are taxed, while a business purchaser can subsequently recover the tax paid on intermediate transactions by offsetting this 'input' tax against the 'output' tax remitted to the authorities. The net effect, for transactions between VAT-registered traders, is to relieve intermediate transactions of any tax burden, and the tax on goods sold to final consumers is then solely determined by the rate of tax applicable on the final sale.[10]

A simple numerical example can illustrate the close equivalence between RST and VAT (Figure 4.1). The example calculates the application of RST and VAT to a two-firm chain of production. Firm A produces an intermediate good, all of which is sold to Firm B, for use as inputs to production. Firm B's output consists entirely of goods sold to final consumers. The goods produced by Firm A are subject to a tax rate of 13 per cent, while the goods produced by Firm B are subject to a tax rate of 20 per cent. It will be seen that, as a result of the credit which Firm B receives for the input VAT it paid on purchased intermediate goods, the net amount of tax revenue collected ($80,000) is the same with VAT as with RST. The tax burden on the final product is in both cases determined by the tax rate applicable to the final goods, and the VAT rate applied to the sale of the intermediate good does not affect this.

Total value added (sales minus the cost of purchased intermediate goods) is equal to $200,000 in both firms. In the example shown, the VAT rates applicable

---

[10] A detailed account of the properties and operation of VAT is provided by Ebrill et al. (2001).

	Firm A	Firm B
Total sales (before tax)	200,000	400,000
Sales to final consumers	0	400,000
Sales to other firms	200,000	0
Purchased intermediate goods	0	200,000
Value Added Tax (VAT)		
VAT rate applied to sales	13%	20%
Total VAT on sales	0.13 x 200,000 = 26,000	0.20 x 400,000 = 80,000
Credit for VAT paid on inputs	0	−26,000
Net VAT bill	26,000	54,000
Retail Sales Tax (RST)		
RST rate applied to retail sales	13%	20%
Retail sales	0	400,000
RST on retail sales	0	80,000

Figure 4.1 Illustration of VAT and RST applied to a two-firm chain of production

to the goods sold by the two firms happened to differ. If, on the other hand, the goods sold by Firm A were subject to the same VAT rate, 20 per cent, as applied to the goods sold by Firm B, then the net VAT bill of Firm A would be $40,000. Since these sales are all made to Firm B, which can offset the VAT paid on its inputs against its VAT liability on sales, the net VAT collected from Firm B would fall from $54,000 to $40,000. Overall, the total amount of VAT collected would be unchanged, at $80,000. However, it will be noted that in this special case where the VAT rate applicable to the goods sold by the two firms is the same, the VAT paid by each firm would be proportional to its value added. This is the only sense in which the tax is related to value added; in other respects the term 'value added tax' is, strictly speaking, a misnomer.

An important distinction in a VAT system is between trades that are VAT-exempt, and those that are 'zero-rated'. If firms are VAT-exempt, their sales are untaxed, but they are also unable to recover the VAT paid on purchased intermediate goods. As a result, their sales are liable to bear some rate of 'effective' VAT, in the form of the unrecovered input VAT, even though their output is untaxed. By contrast, a trader selling goods that are zero-rated charges a VAT rate of zero on the sale, but can still recover VAT on any purchased intermediate goods.

Typically, any system of retail sales taxation faces a trade-off between the costs and effectiveness of enforcement. Although RST and VAT generate the same total revenue from a given set of transactions, with a retail sales tax, all of the revenue is collected from the firms making retail sales. In the example, all the RST revenue is collected from Firm B, and Firm A, which makes no sales to final consumers, has no RST liability. With VAT, tax collection is spread across all the firms in the chain of production. Part of the VAT revenue is collected from Firm A, and a smaller amount is collected from Firm B than under RST. The advantage of spreading tax payments across a larger number of firms in this way is that it may reduce incentives for evasion, and hence strengthen the rate of tax compliance. Under an RST, if Firm B reports sales of zero, all indirect tax revenue from this chain of production is lost. By contrast, with a VAT, the firm may to a certain extent be inhibited in its ability to claim back all of the VAT on its inputs by the need to report a plausible relationship between its inputs and outputs, so that if Firm B reports sales of zero, the maximum gain it can make from this fraud against the tax authorities is $54,000. Where firms have a higher ratio of inputs to sales value (which would often be the case for retail firms), the incentive for evasion may be reduced quite appreciably, compared with the situation with RST. It is exaggerating matters to claim, as some have done, that VAT is 'self-enforcing', because VAT-registered firms would always want to have documentary evidence, in the form of a VAT invoice showing the tax they have paid on their purchases, so that they can reclaim the VAT from the tax authorities. Certainly, this feature of the VAT diminishes the extent to which VAT-registered firms might wish to trade with 'shadow economy' suppliers offering untaxed goods and services, but there are still various ways in which unscrupulous firms could profitably undertake such transactions. However, the fact that, with VAT, the collection of taxes is more widely spread across firms than with an equivalent retail sales tax – and, on average, less per taxed firm – may reduce the incentive for evasion, while the involvement of firms selling intermediate goods with the tax authorities may provide the authorities with further information which may be useful in enforcement. Offsetting this, of course, the revenue authorities have the task of dealing with more taxpaying firms, and this could increase the costs of tax administration.

If many small traders must be taxed, the administrative and enforcement costs of indirect taxes can be high in relation to revenues. One significant advantage of VAT is that it may be possible to reduce administrative costs at relatively low cost in terms of foregone revenue by exempting small traders from VAT obligations. Because VAT-exempt firms cannot recover the VAT paid on inputs, their output still bears an effective rate of VAT. Consequently the net loss to the revenue authorities is significantly reduced, as compared with exempting equivalent small retailers under a retail sales tax.

The choice of the turnover threshold below which small firms are not required to register for VAT becomes one of the key policy parameters in the cost-effective operation of VAT, and the factors that should be weighed up in setting the threshold have been discussed by Keen and Mintz (2004). Their calculations, based on a fixed distribution of firm sizes and plausible parameter values, indicated an optimal threshold towards the upper end of the range encountered in EU member states.

The size distribution of firms does, however, appear to exhibit some 'bunching', just below the turnover at which firms are required to register for VAT, which suggests that firm size might be endogenous, in the sense that firms might hold their output just below the VAT threshold, even if their efficient scale of activity would be higher. Firms may wish to do so to avoid any fixed compliance costs of entering the VAT system, and because of the discontinuity in tax liability at the registration threshold: once registered, the firm is liable to pay VAT on all turnover, and not just on turnover above the threshold. If firm size is endogenous to the VAT turnover threshold, Keen and Mintz show that the optimal threshold could be substantially higher than when calculated assuming a fixed distribution of firm sizes.

5 VAT and Financial Services

The literature on VAT often treats financial services as a special case. How the VAT, or the broader indirect tax system, should deal with financial services is an unsettled issue. The exemption of many financial services from value added taxes has prompted discussions of whether and how financial services should be taxed. The issue has two aspects. One is whether, in principle, financial services should be subject to VAT on the same basis as other goods and services according to theoretical principles or whether there are arguments for taxing some or all categories of financial services differently from the general rate of VAT. The other question is whether, in practice, there exist operational ways to levy such taxes. It is a widespread view in policy documents, public debate, and parts of the academic literature that failure to tax financial services creates distortions on the grounds that financial services are being tax favoured compared to other goods and services. As stated by Jack (2000, p. 841): 'Most authors take as given the desirability of taxing financial services, and confine themselves to implementation issues.' According to this view, our main task should be to search for feasible mechanisms for taxing financial services. Where a standard VAT (usually referred to as the credit-invoice method) is found impracticable, one should search for an operable proxy.

The underlying argument is simple. When most commodities are taxed, exempting some will create distortions by inducing substitution from taxed to untaxed goods and services. A caveat is that when the tax-exempt sector purchases inputs on which a VAT is charged, this VAT will be embedded in the sales price of the commodities supplied by the sector. When the tax-exempt sector itself delivers an intermediate good, a VAT is added to the price in later stages of the production and trade chain. Then any tax on the purchased inputs will be part of the tax base in later stages and VAT will be imposed on VAT: this is known as cascading. The prevailing view is therefore that financial services are tax favoured when delivered to consumers and over-taxed when delivered to businesses, in turn implying over-taxation of the final commodities in which these intermediate goods are embedded. A further distortion is the incentive for tax-exempt businesses to choose in-house production rather than outsourcing even when the former is more costly, since a tax saving is obtained.

The existing academic literature conveys mixed conclusions regarding taxation of financial services. Grubert and Mackie (2000) question whether an explicit tax on financial services is justified, and, referring to a variety of financial services, they write: 'We find that if the government fully taxes all direct consumption of goods and services, then also taxing these financial services will distort the consumer's decisions.' A recurring argument in their discussion is that financial services are not consumption goods that directly yield the consumer utility. Boadway and Keen (2003) dismiss this argument saying that 'there are many other items that are commonly taxed, or recommended to be so, even though they too are clearly not final objects of utility'. In a widely cited paper, Auerbach and Gordon (2002) argue that 'in principle, the VAT should apply to resources devoted to financial transactions in the same way as it does in other sectors'. The essence of the argument is that acquiring a unit of a consumption good requires both a production cost and a transaction cost due to financial services. To achieve efficient use of resources it is necessary to tax both cost components in order not to distort relative costs facing the consumers.

In the following sections, we shall discuss the taxation of some specific[11] financial services, mainly leaving aside the practical aspects of these taxes.

5.1 Financial Intermediation

An important category of financial services is financial intermediation facilitating savings and borrowing. To address main features of these financial services, we take as our point of departure a framework that is close to a simple model in Boadway and Keen (2003). To establish a benchmark, we assume that the representative consumer earns an exogenous income in period j (=1,2). First-period income can be used for consumption and (positive or negative) savings.

---

[11] We have had to be selective and have left out for instance payment services. For a recent analysis, see Lockwood and Yerushalmi (2019).

In the second period, the exogenous income plus interest and first-period savings are used for consumption. Also assume that the consumer incurs a fixed cost in each period, charged by a financial institution (bank) when the consumer establishes a bank account or takes a loan. There is a fixed rate of return to capital, i, say in the world market, and a fixed transaction cost in the banking sector per unit of savings or borrowing. The transaction cost may arise because savings require employment in the financial sector the opportunity cost of which is output of consumption goods foregone. The interest rate facing the consumer is then the gross return minus the transaction cost per unit of savings. Denote by ρ_i the interest rate inclusive of transaction costs in the case of borrowing ($i = B$) and net of transaction costs in the case of positive savings ($i = S$); $\rho_B > i > \rho_S$. The differences $\rho_B - i$ and $i - \rho_S$ then reflect transaction costs. The consumer has preferences over first- and second-period consumption.

As is well known, a consumption tax with a fixed tax rate, τ, over time does not distort the intertemporal allocation. The social rate of return on savings net of the transaction cost is ρ_S. Saving one unit of income in the first period, the consumer foregoes $1/(1+\tau)$ units of consumption and obtains $(1+\rho_S)/(1+\tau)$ additional units of consumption in period 2. The return per unit of consumption foregone is $1+\rho_S$, which is equal to the social return. There is no distortion. A tax on the transaction cost embedded in the rate of return – a so-called margin-based fee – will lead to a downward distortion of positive savings as the private return diminishes. Analogously, a tax on the transaction cost will imply a downward distortion of borrowing as the private cost of borrowing increases. Taxes on fixed fees will not affect the marginal trade-offs and cause no distortions. These insights prompted Boadway and Keen[12] to infer that the spread charge should be left untaxed, and to conclude: 'Financial services charged for as a fixed fee should be taxed'. This conclusion is referred to as 'a simple benchmark for policy'.

While a tax on the fixed costs is harmless from a social efficiency perspective in the aforementioned model, there seems to be no reason why the tax would indeed be strictly beneficial. Where a direct lump-sum tax is available (as at least one element of the tax system) there is no reason also to impose a tax on the fees charged by financial institutions for fixed costs. However, whether these costs are indeed incurred may be endogenous. In Boadway and Keen, the fixed cost is a cost of acquiring a savings account allowing the consumer to save up for the next period. This means that the benefits from savings must be large enough to outweigh this cost. Where this is the case with a small margin, a tax

---

[12] Boadway and Keen (2003), p. 62.

may reverse the decision to save, and there is a tax distortion of savings behaviour. A tax on this cost is no longer a lump sum tax. A further concern may be that a tax on the 'fixed' fee may induce substitution from fixed fees to margin-based fees.

This analysis assesses potential financial taxes against a first-best benchmark. This is an important first step as it sheds light on the claim often made that absence of taxes on financial services causes distortions. In practice, further analysis is required to allow for second-best considerations. Since it is common to tax capital income and to grant deductions of interest on debt, it is of interest to consider coexistence of capital income taxation and a potential tax on financial intermediation.

We now turn to an optimal tax approach where income is treated as endogenous. We set up the following model, which is a version of the Corlett–Hague model (Corlett and Hague, 1953). We consider a representative agent in two periods, indexed 1 and 2, respectively. The agent consumes in both periods and works in one or both periods. S is savings in the first period where $S \geq 0$ or $S < 0$. In either case the consumer will be charged with the administrative cost of saving or borrowing (cost of intermediation services).

The agent is assumed to supply an amount h of labour which is remunerated by a wage rate w_1 in period 1 and by w_2 in period 2. We may assume that there is a fixed division of labour between the periods, including the special cases that labour is supplied only in one of the periods (i.e. $w_1 = 0$ or $w_2 = 0$). The utility function of the agent is $u(C_1, C_2, h)$. There is a VAT rate τ and a tax rate t on interest (with interest on debt being deductible). Denote the interest rate by ρ. The budget constraints are $w_1 h = (1 + \tau)C_1 + S$ and $(1 + \tau)C_2 = w_2 h + (1 + \rho - t\rho)S$, and the intertemporal budget constraint is then $(1 + \tau)C_2 = w_2 h + (1 + \rho - t\rho)\left(w_1 h - (1 + \tau)C_1\right)$. It follows that the indirect utility function can be written $V\left((1 + \rho - t\rho)(1 + \tau), (1 + \tau), (1 + \rho - t\rho)w_1 + w_2\right)$ where the three arguments can be interpreted as the price of C_1, the price of C_2, and the total wage rate assigned to h, respectively.

The agent will be charged for the intermediation cost (including tax if any) through a higher interest if borrowing and a lower interest if lending. The optimal tax problem is to maximize utility subject to the tax revenue requirement. Carrying out the optimization, we can show the following result: *When there is an optimal tax on interest imposing VAT on the financial service makes no difference.* (For further analytical details, see Christiansen, 2017.)

Here we have assumed that the tax on interest is set based on a simple intertemporal model. In practice, there may be other concerns involved. If it is considered desirable to discourage borrowing, this could be done by lowering t

to diminish the effect of interest deductibility. If this is difficult due to other concerns, there may be a case for abolishing the VAT exemption. A case may be where the rate of the capital income tax t is linked to the tax rate on profits (as in Norway) so that a lower t, unlike a tax on the intermediation services, will imply a more lenient taxation of profits.

Lockwood (2015) analyses taxation of financial intermediation services in a model where heterogeneous firms borrow from banks. The key finding is that a tax on intermediation will distort the efficient allocation of capital across firms, and so this tax is optimally set to zero in accordance with the Diamond–Mirrlees production efficiency theorem.

Empirical analyses of indirect taxation of financial services are sparse. A rare example is Büttner and Erbe (2014), who analyse the revenue and welfare effects of abolishing the VAT exemption of financial services in Germany. Their analysis takes into account the full input–output structure of the economy as well as labour supply responses. Imposing revenue neutrality by adjusting the standard VAT rate, they find that repealing the VAT exemption yields a modest welfare gain.

5.2 Insurance

Let us next consider insurance services. By buying insurance, agents become entitled to a compensation in the event of a loss if a bad state occurs. We shall assume that the insurer charges the insured for the cost of providing insurance services through a loading factor in the insurance premium. A question is then whether one should impose a tax, say VAT, on this transaction cost. As a framework for addressing this issue, we shall use a model close to the one employed in Grubert and Mackie (2000) and Jack (2000), but the analysis will be extended somewhat beyond theirs.

We consider an individual with a resource endowment Y. To establish a non-distorted benchmark, we assume that some of it may be taxed away by a lump-sum tax, T. Two contingencies exist. With probability $1 - \pi$, the agent will experience a good state where $Y - T$ can be used for consumption, C_g. With probability π, the agent will experience a bad state where he or she loses L of the endowment and will only have $Y - L - T$ available for consumption, C_b, unless some compensation scheme is in place. In this case, there is a general loss of purchasing power, which could be considered as a loss of earnings ability or even as loss of household earnings due to the death of a breadwinner, as in the case of life insurance.[13] We shall consider a different case at the end of the section.

---

[13] In practice, life insurance would include a savings component abstracted from in the present context. This was a central issue in Barham et al. (1987).

We assume that initially agents are identical and normalize the population to unity. In general, distributional concerns are crucial in discussions of optimal taxation, which typically involves a trade-off between distribution and social efficiency. However, in the interest of a focussed discussion of efficiency, we neglect agent heterogeneity and distribution in the current context. The debate about taxation of financial services has mainly been concerned with efficiency considerations (i.e. whether taxation or missing taxation improves or distorts the resource allocation). This issue is relevant regardless of concerns with distribution and can be discussed in a homogenous agent framework.

Now consider a transfer from the good state to the bad state, which takes the form of an insurance premium P in both states used to finance a compensation, C, in the bad state. Moreover, assume that there is a real cost k per unit transferred implying a total cost kC, which we can think of as the value added created by an insurer. Then

$$P = (1+k)C\pi,$$

where k is known as a loading factor. We denote by τ the consumption tax rate, which we can think of as a value added tax even if our simple model does not distinguish between different types of consumption taxes as we neglect purchases of intermediate goods. Where the input–output structure is taken into account, it makes a difference whether there is a 'proper' value added tax granting a refund of the tax paid on purchased intermediate goods or whether one simply imposes a tax on the value added without any refund.[14] Even if leaving aside some characteristics of the value added tax, the model is sufficient to address the key question raised in the debate over whether a value added tax exempting financial services distorts the consumption bundle. To focus sharply on this issue, we also abstract from other distortions such as labour supply distortions, which is the reason why we assume an exogenous resource endowment.

Then the budget constraints in the respective states are

$$(1+\tau)C_g = Y - T - (1+k)C\pi$$

and

$$(1+\tau)C_b = Y - T - L - (1+k)C\pi + C$$

A one-unit increase of consumption in the bad state requires an increase in the compensation equal to $dC = (1 + \tau)/\left(1 - (1 + k)\pi\right)$, implying a change of consumption in the good state equal to $dC_g = -(1 + k)\pi/\left(1 - (1 + k)\pi\right)$, which shows the cost in the good state of additional consumption in the bad state. The important observation is now that this cost is independent of the consumption tax and consequently the same as in the pure lump sum tax regime. A value added tax exempting insurance services generates the same allocation as a lump sum tax. If one were to impose a tax on the cost of financial services, kC, one would distort the trade-off between consumption in the two states compared to the lump-sum tax regime. Nonetheless, there may be scope for improving the allocation. The reason is that due to the loading factor there is less than full insurance, which means that further insurance would be welfare enhancing. One way to achieve this might be to subsidize insurance. One could finance the subsidy by increasing the general VAT to keep tax revenue unchanged, at least as long as there is no change in C. The reason is simple. The general VAT will impose a larger tax burden in the good state where consumption, and hence the tax base, is larger, while the insurance subsidy will grant the same benefit in both states. It follows that more of the tax burden is shifted from the bad state to the good state, which is beneficial from the perspective of the risk-averse taxpayer.

Besides this 'mechanical' effect, there may be behavioural effects on the acquisition of insurance. By lowering the marginal cost of insurance, the subsidy may have a stimulating effect. On the other hand. there may be a counteracting effect as the mitigation of risk through subsidies and taxes may discourage the private acquisition of insurance.

As is common in optimal tax analysis, we have neglected any administrative cost of taxation. However, it seems plausible that introducing a novel tax or subsidy will involve a cost. An immediate implication is a further erosion of any argument for a tax on insurance. Clearly, the cost will also weaken the case for a subsidy, implying that the benefits from a subsidy must outweigh the administrative cost in order to be worthwhile. The most robust policy conclusion from our analysis is therefore that there is hardly a case for imposing a positive tax on the kind of insurance addressed here. There may be a case for introducing a subsidy, which, however, is less compelling in the presence of administrative costs.

Let us now consider a different case. Rather than considering the loss of a general endowment or income, we look at property insurance, that is, insurance against the loss of a particular good. How in principle one would like to deal with the various aspects of taxes on property insurance has not been much discussed in the literature. Barham et al. (1987) focus on VAT on the item being insured, assuming costless provision of intermediation services, but argue in general that 'the intermediation service provided by insurances companies is what should be taxed' (p. 181).

To address property insurance, we retain the assumption that there is a population of identical individuals normalized at unity. Now consider a case where agents can expend resources on two goods, one of which can be lost or damaged. For simplicity, we consider a (total) loss. There is a resource endowment Y available for acquiring the goods. We consider the following setting. An agent buys B units of the good that can be lost and X units of the other good. The unit cost of both commodities is set equal to unity. An agent can also purchase insurance guaranteeing that C units will be available even if there is a loss of the initial quantity. A loss occurs with probability π. To be guaranteed that a unit is available, possibly after a series of losses, $\rho = \frac{1}{1-\pi}$ units must be acquired per agent.[15] The transaction cost of paying compensation to the insured is $(1 + \tau)k\rho C$ where k is a positive constant and $(1 + \tau)C$ is the indemnity enabling the agent to buy C units when the tax-inclusive price is $(1 + \tau)$. The total insurance premium is then $\pi(1 + k)\rho C(1 + \tau)$. Full insurance would imply $C = B$.

An individual derives utility $u(X)$ from X and utility $v(B)$ from B. Both functions are assumed to be increasing and strictly concave. The budget constraint is

$$Y = (1 + \tau)X + (1 + \tau)B + \pi(1 + k)\rho(1 + \tau)C + T,$$

where T is a lump sum tax. The resource endowment is used for buying X, B, and insurance and paying the tax. We then have that X is received with certainty, while B is received when loss is avoided with probability $1 - \pi$, and $(1 + \tau)C$ is the indemnity enabling the agent to buy C units when the after-tax price is $(1 + \tau)C$.

Alternatively, we can rewrite the budget constraint as

$$X = \frac{Y}{1 + \tau} - B - \pi(1 + k)\rho C - \frac{T}{1 + \tau}.$$

Then the expected utility is

$$u(X) + (1 - \pi)v(B) + \pi v(C) = u\left(\frac{Y}{1 + \tau} - B - \pi(1 + k)\rho C - \frac{T}{1 + \tau}\right)$$
$$+ (1 - \pi)v(B) + \pi v(C).$$

---

[15] Note that $\frac{\pi}{1-\pi}$ is the sum of an infinite geometric series of losses that arises when a fraction π of the first unit is lost, a fraction π of the replacement is lost, and so on ad infinitum. $\rho = 1 + \frac{\pi}{1-\pi}$.

Maximizing wrt B and C we get the first order conditions

$$-u' + (1 - \pi)v'(B) = 0$$

and

$$-u'\pi(1 + k)\rho + \pi v'(C) = 0.$$

It follows that

$$v'(B)(1 + k) = v'(C)$$

and $C \leq B$ according as $k \geq 0$. There is full insurance when there is no transaction cost and partial insurance when there is a strictly positive transaction cost.

We observe that the chosen allocation is the same regardless of whether taxation relies on a lump sum tax or a value added tax exempting financial services (i.e. not imposing a tax on $k\rho C$).

This presentation has neglected a number of aspects of value added taxation and insurance. It has been assumed that there is no tax on insurance when the services of insurance companies are tax exempt. However, there is an implicit tax when insurance companies buy inputs from other sectors, and the VAT on these intermediate goods are not refundable when the sector is VAT exempt. Another aspect of the input–output structure is that VAT exemption introduces a bias in favour of in-house production rather than outsourcing of activities needed for producing the output of insurance companies, or any other tax-exempt business.

We have addressed insurance purchased by consumers, but buying insurance can also be part of business activities. For instance, equipment used in firms can break down due to some random event. For businesses insuring their property, insurance is an intermediate good that should be left untaxed according to the Diamond–Mirrlees production efficiency theorem.

In many cases, producers provide what is equivalent to insurance for the customers by offering a warranty guaranteeing that if a purchased item breaks down the producer will replace it free of charge. Processing claims and administering this guarantee, the seller will incur a cost, which must be covered by a mark-up of the price on which a value added tax is levied. A VAT-exempt insurance company will then have a tax advantage over firms offering warranties. This distortion may induce a social inefficiency where insurance through warranties is underprovided. A question is whether a company specializing in insurance or a firm with specialized knowledge about the particular item it produces is the more efficient insurer. However, efficient form of insurance may not be the key issue. The reason why a firm offers a warranty is usually that the producer wants to signal that the item is of good quality when the customers cannot directly observe its properties. Important and related questions are then whether the optimal quality is produced and whether warranties or the terms of conventional insurance contracts more adequately convey information about quality.

5.3 Currency Trade

As a final example of financial services, we shall briefly consider currency trade, which is interesting per se, but also illustrates some general insights. We suppose a VAT-registered firm imports a good at a foreign price p. Let the exchange rate be v and suppose the cost of currency exchange is kp. If the currency trader is tax exempt, he charges kp and the import price including the cost of the financial service is $vp + kp$. Denote by b the cost (value added) of the activities carried out by the importer. Charging VAT when selling the good to a consumer, the importer will charge the tax-inclusive price $(1 + \tau)(vp + kp + b)$. There is the same tax mark-up of the price as for other (domestically provided) goods.

If the currency trader charges VAT, he pays τkp to the tax office and charges $(1 + \tau)kp$. The importer incurs a tax-inclusive cost $vp + (1 + \tau)kp + b$. τkp is refunded and the net cost faced by the importer is $vp + kp + b$. The importer charges the tax-inclusive price $(1 + \tau)(vp + kp + b)$. It makes no difference whether the currency trader is tax exempt or not. If the currency trader does not charge VAT, the importer will add VAT to the consumer price. If the currency trader charges VAT, the importer will get a refund and add VAT to the consumer price. The only difference is who remits the VAT on the currency trade. This illustrates the more general insight that if there is a first stage of the production and distribution chain only delivering intermediate goods, it makes no difference whether it is tax exempt or not.

A different case arises when currency exchange is a service purchased by consumers to be able to travel or do shopping abroad. Consumers will then directly import many goods and services from abroad on which no home country VAT is paid. Since VAT is levied on domestic goods and commercial imports, the missing VAT on cross-border shopping will create a distortion. As a partial taxation of consumers' purchases abroad, VAT on currency exchange is therefore, in principle, efficiency enhancing but presumably with a minor quantitative impact.

6 International Aspects of Indirect Taxation

In principle, there are many ways in which indirect tax policies of one country could have effects that are felt beyond its boundaries – including effects on the level and pattern of economic activity in other countries, on the pattern of international trade, savings, and investment, on other countries' tax revenues, and on the tax policy choices that they in turn might make. In order not to excessively broaden the scope of this Element, we shall leave aside several effects including the effects of tariffs or tariff-equivalent effects of indirect taxes.

6.1 Origin vs Destination Sales Taxes

Where goods and services are traded between countries, questions arise as to where and on what basis indirect taxes should be applied. In very general terms, we could contrast an 'origin' regime under which indirect taxes are levied in the country of production with a 'destination' regime where indirect taxes are levied in the country of consumption.

In practice, a retail sales tax system naturally tends towards the destination basis for indirect taxation. A tax imposed on sales to final consumers will generally be levied in the country of consumption, except where there is cross-border shopping by individuals. VAT systems generally include tax adjustments on internationally traded goods and services, so that the net outcome is broadly consistent with a destination basis for taxation. Usually this outcome is achieved by zero-rating exported goods (i.e. charging a tax rate of zero on the sale, while also allowing the seller to recover the costs of VAT incurred on the purchase of intermediate goods), and imposing VAT on the full value of imported goods.

We discuss the distinctive issues relating to the VAT treatment of traded goods in Section 6.2. For the remainder of the current section, we avoid the complications arising from taxed transactions in intermediate goods, and our discussion can perhaps be best interpreted with reference to a simplified world in which a sales tax can be applied at the end of a single-stage production activity, either by the country where production takes place, or by the country where the consumer lives.

Although most systems of indirect taxation operate a destination-basis treatment of internationally traded goods, it is not wholly clear that this is required for economic efficiency. Indeed, it may perhaps seem odd that much attention is given to the adjustment of sales taxes for goods traded across borders when countries maintain – and make no corresponding adjustment to – large differences in payroll taxes and other taxes that feed into the cost of production. Moreover, there is a theoretical literature which indicates that under certain conditions it makes no difference whether sales taxes are levied on a destination basis or an origin basis. Given these conditions, a sales tax levied on an origin basis (i.e. in the exporting country) would have the same economic effects as a tax levied on a destination basis, even where the tax rates levied by countries differ.

A clear account of the mechanism is given in Lockwood et al. (1994a), but the gist of the argument runs as follows: In a two-country, single-period model with perfect competition, where each country applies a single percentage sales tax rate to all goods and services, the country applying the higher tax rate would have a lower exchange rate under the destination principle than under the origin principle, just sufficient to offset the tax differential, leaving real incomes, the allocation of revenues, and the allocation of productive activity unchanged.

The conditions that underpin this neutrality result have been explored in a number of papers; see, for example, Crawford et al., 2010. For neutrality to hold between sales taxes levied on an origin basis and a destination basis, the requirement that each country should apply a single tax rate to all sales is crucial. Where countries apply different tax rates to different goods and services, the exchange rate adjustment can only exactly offset the tax differences between countries in the special case described by Fratianni and Christie (1981) where one country's tax rates on goods are higher than the other country's by a constant proportional factor. Even in this special case, the allocation of revenues between countries is likely to differ, and equivalence between the destination and origin bases of taxation could only be achieved with some revenue redistribution between the two countries (Keen and Smith, 1996).

Assuming a single-period economy ensures that trade between the two countries is balanced, so that aggregate consumption equals aggregate production in each economy. Since origin-based taxation taxes the value of production and destination-based taxation taxes the value of aggregate consumption, the balanced trade assumption ensures that the tax base is the same under the two regimes. A similar equality between aggregate consumption and aggregate production can also hold in net present value terms in a multi-period economy (Keen 1993). However, as Bovenberg (1994) points out, the shift of tax base between production and consumption would have significant intergenerational implications, and potential effects on the incentives for savings and capital accumulation.

Moving beyond the two-country context adds further conditions about uniformity of treatment across different countries; each country should systematically apply either the destination principle or the origin principle to all their trading partners. This requirement appears to conflict with the idea, discussed by Shibata (1967), that countries which are members of a customs union would naturally apply the origin basis to trade between union members, while they might wish to apply a destination-basis treatment to trade with the rest of the world – the so-called 'restricted origin principle'. In this context, there is no guarantee of balanced trade flows between the groups of countries subject to the different bases of taxation, even in a single-period model; moreover, there would be incentives for trade deflection (routing exports via a third country to exploit the differences in the basis of taxation). In an intriguing paper, Lockwood et al. (1994b) show that in this case neutrality can be restored if the customs union members apply taxation on the origin basis systematically to *all* their trade, despite the fact that their partners in the rest of the world apply a different basis – a neat solution, albeit one that has the severe presentational drawback that some trades would be taxed twice, while others not at all.

In addition to the aforementioned rather restrictive conditions for equivalence between the destination and origin bases for a given pattern of tax rates, a change from one basis to the other would also alter the tax-setting incentives of governments. Under the origin basis for sales taxation, countries can attract additional tax base by undercutting the tax rates of their competitors, while no corresponding incentive arises under destination-based sales taxation. In addition, where a country is large enough to influence world market prices, it would face differing incentives to exploit this market power under the two regimes. These different tax-setting incentives are a further reason to believe that the choice between origin and destination bases for taxation is one of real economic substance rather than broad equivalence.

Unfortunately, it is difficult to reach clear conclusions about which regime – destination or origin – should, in principle, be preferred. Keen and Smith (1996) provide an extensive survey of the issues. The natural starting point might seem to be the result of Diamond and Mirrlees (1971), that a Pareto-efficient tax system should exhibit production efficiency, avoiding distortion of intermediate goods transactions, and levying distortive revenue-raising taxes only on sales to final consumers. From this perspective, a destination basis for indirect taxation, which ensures production efficiency in the sense of taxing goods produced in different countries at the same rate, would appear superior to an origin basis, in which production in different countries could be taxed at different rates. However, Keen and Smith point out that the Diamond and Mirrlees result is not directly applicable to an international context, where individual countries must finance their own revenue requirements; in this context production efficiency will be consistent with Pareto optimality only if revenue transfers can be made between countries to equalize the marginal cost of public funds.

Keen and Smith conclude that the theoretical arguments point less decisively in favour of a destination basis for indirect taxation than had at one time been supposed, but, nevertheless, there seems to be no compelling theoretical case for preferring an origin basis. In terms of practical policy, perhaps the most compelling argument is that made by Cnossen and Shoup (1987) in reviewing the relative merits of the origin and destination principles for indirect taxation in the EU. Whatever the theoretical arguments, they argue, the destination principle appears to offer businesses engaged in EU-wide competition a level playing field undistorted by national choices in indirect taxation, while an origin basis would be liable to be perceived as inequitable and distorting.

6.2 Origin and Destination VAT

The practical implementation of either the destination principle or the origin principle is substantially more complex where there is a VAT than with a single-stage retail sales tax or excises.

An outcome consistent with the destination principle could be achieved in one of two broad ways:

(1)   by breaking the VAT chain when goods cross national boundaries, so that goods are exported free of VAT, while VAT is applied to imported goods at their full value. Technically the break in the VAT chain is achieved by zero-rating of exports, meaning that no tax is charged on the value of the sale while at the same time the seller is able to recover VAT paid on purchases of intermediate goods. These arrangements mean that none of the past VAT charged on the good remains when it crosses national boundaries, and the VAT chain then starts afresh in the importing country, with the importing country levying VAT at its own rate. The arrangements for VAT on transactions between member states of the EU adopt this approach.

(2)   by continuing the VAT chain across national borders, with the importing country giving credit for the VAT charged in the exporting country. Because the essence of a VAT is that the tax rates on a consumption good are determined by the rate applying to the final transaction, and not by the tax rates applying to earlier, intermediate, transactions, continuing the VAT chain across national borders, and giving full credit for the tax paid in the exporting country, ensures a destination basis outcome in terms of the final tax burden on traded products. As with the zero-rating of exports, an importer sourcing goods from other countries would be indifferent to the rate of VAT levied on their purchases, since they would recover it in due course as an offset against the VAT liability on their own sales. In the late 1980s, a system of this sort was proposed by the European Commission to replace export zero-rating, but never implemented.

Continuing the VAT chain across national borders in this way would lead to an outcome where the tax charged on eventual sales to final consumers is consistent with the destination principle, in that, as with export zero-rating, the tax charged on final sales bears no trace of the tax rates levied in other countries at earlier stages of the chain of production. However, the revenues received by countries would be different to those received under export zero rating, since exporting countries would collect tax on the value of exports, for which credit would then be given by the importing country. The net effect on country revenues would differ depending on the balance of trade and the tax rates applied. It could, of course, be offset by an appropriate revenue adjustment between countries.

The issues raised by VAT adjustments on intra-EU trades are not insignificant practical issues with little economic substance. They affect revenue distribution, evasion opportunities and enforcement incentives – and, in consequence, affect tax rate-setting incentives too. Keen and Smith (1996, 2000) outline an alternative scheme – 'VIVAT' – which they propose as a better compromise between the various deficiencies of the existing system and the proposed EU regime.

One issue which brought the tax adjustments on EU trade under sharp critical scrutiny was the emergence of a serious problem of organized criminal fraud, exploiting the tax adjustments to obtain vast sums in unjustified VAT refunds. While VAT, like all tax regimes, is exposed to the risk of revenue loss through concealed activity and false reporting, the large-scale 'carousel frauds' set up specifically to obtain massive VAT refunds on export transactions, while avoiding paying VAT on corresponding imports, exposed the system to massive revenue losses. Official estimates of the 'VAT gap' in the UK, the revenue shortfall compared with a full-compliance level, peaked at around 17 per cent in 2002–3, compared with less than 10 per cent a decade earlier, with the rapid growth in carousel frauds accounting for much of the increase in the revenue shortfall. Keen and Smith (2006) argue that shifting to a regime which continues the VAT chain across national boundaries would reduce the exposure of the system to criminal fraud.

By contrast to the arrangements for adjusting VAT on trade so as to ensure that the taxation of trade conforms to the destination principle, a genuine origin basis for VAT would be complicated – though not impossible – to achieve. Value added could, of course, be taxed on an origin basis by calculating the value added of each enterprise and taxing this directly, in the relevant country. But if the VAT is to continue in its current shape, as a sales tax with refunding of the VAT paid on business inputs, then the tax adjustments would be complex. Assuming that sales across national boundaries would bear the exporting country's VAT, the 'input VAT' credit that would be given to a business importer would not refund the actual VAT paid in the exporting country, but would instead need to reflect the tax that would hypothetically have been levied had the goods been subject to VAT at the tax rate of the importing country.[16] In principle, such a system could ensure that the VAT charged on goods reflected the tax rates of the countries through which it has passed in the course of manufacture, rather than solely the tax rate of the country of final sale. It is doubtful whether such a system would be well understood, and it is far from clear that there is an economic case strong enough to warrant moving in this direction.

6.3 Cross-Border Shopping

Where consumers can shop abroad and import goods without tax adjustments, differences in commodity tax rates may prompt cross-border shopping by residents of high tax countries in neighbouring lower-tax jurisdictions. With a sufficient tax differential, consumers may be willing to incur the travel costs and inconvenience of cross-border shopping trips; typically it would be expected that people living close to international borders, those making large purchases, and those with a relatively low opportunity cost of time would do more cross-border shopping. The commodities involved will tend to be those – such as alcohol and tobacco products – which are readily transportable and storable, and where the tax differential is greatest.

Cross-border shopping alters the constraints on national tax policy. Crawford and Tanner (1995) discuss the effects of the radical abolition of border controls on travellers between EU member states in 1992, and argue that although this will have increased the tax rate elasticity of tax revenues for highly taxed alcohol and tobacco in the United Kingdom, there was still little indication that tax rates were above the revenue-maximizing level. Christiansen (1994) discusses the effects of cross-border shopping on optimal tax rules, both under perfect and imperfect competition. In the former case, the conventional inverse elasticity rule remains largely unaltered, except that the relevant elasticity is with respect to domestic demand. Where domestic supply comes from a foreign monopoly supplier, Christiansen shows that one effect of cross-border shopping may be to shift part of the tax burden onto the supplier.

Cross-border shopping potentially gives rise to incentives for tax competition, as countries may be tempted to reduce tax rates in order to attract shoppers, and tax revenue, from neighbouring countries, or in order to stem an outflow of such shopping to neighbouring lower-tax locations. It has been suggested that this creates downward pressure on tax rates, and leads to inefficiency in the pattern of revenue raising. Mintz and Tulkens (1986) identify two sources of this inefficiency, in the sense of fiscal externalities which arise when a country

---

[16] See the discussion in Keen and Smith (1996), p. 394.

subject to cross-border shopping changes its tax rate, which they refer to as the public consumption and private consumption externalities, respectively. The first of these arises when country B raises its tax rate, leading to increased sales in neighbouring country A, either because of more cross-border shopping by B's residents in A, or because some of A's residents cease cross-border shopping in B. In either case, tax revenues in A are positively related to B's tax rate. The second externality arises where B has a lower tax rate than A, and is already attracting cross-border shoppers from A. Then, if B raises its tax rate, it imposes a loss in real income on existing cross-border shoppers from A, who have to pay more for each good purchased. Both fiscal externalities create a presumption that the fiscal choices of countries will be set inefficiently in a non-cooperative equilibrium.[17]

In an elegant paper that has sparked an extensive subsequent literature, Kanbur and Keen (1993) show the importance of asymmetries in country (population) size in understanding patterns of tax competition, and in particular the operation of small countries as tax havens. Small countries may experience particularly strong incentives to reduce their sales tax rates below those of neighbouring countries, since the revenue they can gain by cutting taxes to attract additional cross-border shoppers may be large relative to the revenue loss they suffer from the lower tax rate on sales to domestic consumers. Kanbur and Keen go on to assess the welfare properties of possible international measures to constrain tax competition, including harmonization towards the weighted mean of national tax rates (which can never be welfare-improving for the smaller country), and the imposition of a minimum 'floor' tax rate, which in some circumstances may, they suggest, benefit both countries.

In a subsequent paper, Søren Bo Nielsen (2001) models cross-border shopping between countries differing in geographical extent and the effects of various kinds of tax harmonization in this setting. It incorporates costly transportation of goods to the border area to meet the cross-border shoppers' demand and the taxation of profits arising in the border area. The opportunity to make tax-induced profits provides an incentive to stimulate cross-border shopping. A

---

[17] While many (perhaps most) cases of cross-border shopping involve residents of high-tax countries shopping in low-tax countries, cross-border shopping may be motivated by a wider range of factors, including price differences that may exist for various reasons, including some unrelated to taxation. Even then there is a distortion since, for instance, a Norwegian consumer shopping in Sweden will consider the Norwegian tax as a cost, which of course it is privately, but not socially. Suppose the (pre-tax) cost is C and the tax is t in Norway whereas in Sweden the cost is $c < C$ and the tax is s, where s might even be equal to t for the sake of the argument. Suppose the marginal travel and inconvenience cost is k', and $c+s < C+t$. At the equilibrium, $c+s+k' = C+t$. The difference in social cost of cross-border shopping in Sweden is then $c+s+k'-C=t$ since c, s, and k' are real resource costs from a Norwegian perspective. t is then a distorting tax wedge.

further extension is to incorporate the effects of border inspection where cross-border shopping is illegal.

The extent to which cross-border shopping impinges on tax policymaking is limited by the natural convexity that arises from travel and other costs incurred in making journeys for the purpose of cross-border shopping. In general, cross-border shopping is likely to be a phenomenon limited to certain highly taxed, transportable, and storable commodities, and undertaken predominantly by people living in the vicinity of a border with a neighbouring lower-taxed jurisdiction.

Cross-border shopping opportunities are likely to be more extensive, and the constraints placed on tax-setting more severe, where sub-national jurisdictions operate local sales taxes. The US experience, in particular, has provided scope for extensive empirical research on the determinants of cross-border shopping in response to tax differentials. Leal et al. (2010) provide a useful overview of this literature.

Merriman (2010) takes an innovative approach to shed light on the extent of cross-border shopping by observing the proportion of littered cigarette packs in Chicago not displaying a Chicago tax stamp. The probability of a local stamp varies with proximity to a low-tax border.

Agrawal (2015) studies, both theoretically and empirically, cross-border shopping under the coexistence of state and local commodity taxes in the United States. A conclusion is that local taxes will be higher on the low-state-tax side of a border and will depend on proximity to the border. Local taxes will diminish with distance/travel time from the nearest high-tax border and rise when moving away from the nearest low-tax border. A key insight is that a municipality with an inflow of cross-border shoppers can benefit from taxing these consumers locally while those with an outflow of cross-border shoppers due to high own-state taxes will show more restraint in their local tax setting.

Cross-border shopping may also affect the price setting of retailers. Harding et al. (2012) demonstrate that the pass-through of American cigarette taxes to consumer prices depends on distance to borders of states with lower taxes. Where (potential) customers are more likely to acquire lower-taxed cigarettes by engaging in cross-border shopping, retailers face tougher competition and become more reluctant to pass excise taxes through to the consumers. The pass-through rate becomes an increasing function of distance to lower-tax borders.

The development of internet commerce has, however, radically extended the opportunities that people have to make purchases abroad at low cost, without the need for any travel at all. Goods can be ordered from the Internet from sellers abroad, and delivered by courier or the postal service (as of course was already possible with conventional mail-order), and the tax authorities face considerable problems in identifying and levying taxes on goods delivered in this way, especially in the case of small consignments, and across borders where there are no existing customs formalities (as between EU member states, and between states in the United States).[18] More radically, some commodities that were once purchased as physical goods, such as recorded music and films on DVD, are now widely delivered as digital downloads, where the scope for the tax authorities to observe the supply of these commodities is very limited indeed (and where the location of the supplier, and in some cases the customer, is difficult to determine, even in principle). Increasingly, a number of services are also supplied through the Internet, with similar ambiguity about the 'place of supply'.

There has been extensive discussion, especially at international fora such as the OECD, of the bases on which such transactions can and should be taxed.[19] The core principles (as opposed to the methods of implementation) seem to be uncontroversial: Digital services delivered to private consumers should be taxed in the jurisdiction where the customer resides even if the digital services or intangibles may be received in many different places. The OECD has developed guidelines for collection of VAT on online sales. For example, a number of simplifications are recommended to simplify registration and compliance mechanisms, especially for businesses faced with obligations in multiple jurisdictions. The EU has introduced a 'One Stop Shop' scheme, allowing a business making remote sales in multiple jurisdictions to register for VAT purposes in one single place, while levying tax at the rate appropriate to the location of their customers.

Despite the efforts being made to improve compliance and enforcement, we note that in the absence of agreed and implementable principles for the taxation of internet purchases, a significant part of the international supply of some commodities is taxed in low-tax jurisdictions, or escapes taxation entirely. The implications of this are not merely fiscal: Goolsbee et al. (2010) present suggestive evidence of substantial avoidance of excise taxes on cigarettes in the United States through internet purchasing, with obvious implications for health policy. Agrawal (2017) points out that in the United States obligations to remit retail sales taxes depend on whether firms have a nexus in the state. Once a firm has established physical presence in one place in a state, it must remit sales taxes

---

[18] In the case of the United States, the matter is further complicated by constraints on the taxation of inter-state commerce, and by the reluctance of legislators to ensure that internet transactions are taxed on an equivalent basis to other sales (Goolsbee, 2000).

[19] OECD (2015). There are also significant issues about the taxation of corporate profits of enterprises in the digital economy. See, for example, Devereux and Vella (2017).

on online purchases for every town in the state. If online transactions are untaxed in the absence of a nexus, the Internet may put downward pressure on local tax rates. On the other hand, if e-commerce is taxed, the Internet may allow cities and towns to collect taxes on remote transactions that previously went untaxed.

6.4 Duty-Free

A curious economic phenomenon in the field of indirect taxation has been the operation of 'duty-free' provisions for international sea and air travellers, allowing them to buy limited quantities of goods free of indirect taxes. The commodities most involved have been those subject to high rates of excise duty such as alcohol and tobacco products. It is not at all clear in principle why travellers should be singled out for this particular tax privilege, and there have been instances where the deadweight losses provoked by duty-free have been very transparent (including shipping operations in the North Sea that were for some time almost entirely sustained by the business generated by travellers wishing to benefit from duty-free).

Duty-free trade raises a number of issues that are interesting from the perspectives of positive and normative economics. Christiansen and Smith (2001) argue that duty-free can be thought of as a revenue-raising mechanism with distinctive properties, rather than as the complete absence of taxation. Depending on market structure, the rent earned by duty-free traders may be substantial, and governments may be able to capture some of this rent through various mechanisms. By auctioning a limited number of duty-free concessions, for example, a government may recover much of the tax revenue apparently foregone by permitting duty-free sales.

They set out a simple baseline model of duty-free competition, to explore the processes of competition in the duty-free market, both between market partici-pants and between governments. They note two distinctive features of the duty-free market: the presence of transactions costs or quantity restrictions which limit the scale of duty-free purchases, and the fact that duty-free purchases are essentially joint purchases of two things, the duty-free commodity and travel. They note in particular the significance of transaction costs in limiting what they describe as 'cross-hauling', that is, purchases of duty-free goods on the outward leg of a journey, which are then brought back on the return journey for consumption at home. If cross-hauling is sufficiently inconvenient, duty-free pricing may reflect competition from high-street retailers at both ends of the journey, but not from duty-free operators at other airports.

The EU abolished duty-free on intra-EU journeys in 1999. Duty-free sales on intra-EU travel had increasingly been recognized as anachronistic. Some forms of travel between member states benefited from duty-free while others did not. The EU's coordinated abolition of internal duty-free was controversial, and the target of a well-resourced lobbying campaign, right up until the date of implementation. Christiansen and Smith (2004) explore the pattern of individual country interests in the maintenance of duty-free. While duty-free may be globally inefficient, individual country interests differ, and high-tax countries, in particular, may lose from abolition if they lose the revenues from licensing duty-free franchises, and if the duty-free sales are replaced by high-street sales in lower-tax countries.

Christiansen and Smith (2008) consider one particular tax policy aspect of duty-free, namely its implications for optimal commodity taxation. Systems of revenue-raising commodity taxation typically suffer from the limitation that the same tax structure is offered to all consumers, whatever their demand characteristics. However, individuals differ in their opportunities to benefit from duty-free shopping, and Christiansen and Smith (2008) explore the implications of these differences for optimal commodity taxation within a Mirrlees-type optimal tax model. In this context, duty-free provides the opportunity to offer individuals different commodity tax schedules, with potentially welfare-improving results.

7 Using Indirect Taxes to Achieve Changes in Behaviour

While most indirect taxes have been levied to raise revenue, sales taxes on some commodities have been deployed explicitly with the aim of achieving socially desired shifts in behaviour.

This has been the rationale for 'green taxes', which aim to shift production and/or consumption away from environmentally harmful commodities (Section 7.1). A similar objective may partly underlie the very high rates of excise duty (or 'sin taxes') imposed on alcoholic drinks and tobacco products in many countries (Section 7.2).

The notion that one should tax harmful consumption has various justifications. Pigou (1920) showed how taxes could be used to reflect social costs that market agents would otherwise not take into account, thereby internalizing negative externalities. The basic theory of such Pigouvian or externality-correcting taxes is quite simple: by setting taxes equal to the marginal external cost, the first-best real allocation is achieved (Baumol, 1972). However, in practice a number of constraints and complications arise: the economy is distorted in various ways, and not all sources of externalities can be taxed in an ideal way (Sandmo, 1995, 2000; Fullerton et al., 2010).

Other arguments for taxing harmful consumption reflect the notion of merit goods, which are sometimes seen as an argument for 'paternalistic' policy interventions, overriding the consumer's own preferences or judgements, often on the basis that people may be poorly informed about the consequences of certain choices. A recent development in the literature, which we discuss in Section 7.3, has been analyses of individual behaviour that allow for the possibility that individuals may make choices that may not be in their own best interests, for a wider set of reasons than limited information.

7.1 Taxes and Externalities

In environmental policy, there has been increasing interest in the use of incentive-based approaches to environmental regulation, for example, through emissions trading or carbon taxes to discourage the use of fossil fuels.

What these approaches have in common is the desire to avoid the rigidity and excessive costs associated with more conventional approaches to environmental policy, such as regulations, which impose limits on emissions, or require the use of particular pollution-control technologies. Where polluters differ in the costs they incur in reducing emissions, using incentive mechanisms such as emission taxes to discourage emissions may achieve a given reduction in emissions at lower total cost, by encouraging greater abatement by those polluters able to reduce emissions at low cost, while allowing polluters that would incur excessive abatement costs to pay the tax instead (Kneese and Bower, 1968; Newell and Stavins, 2003) – the so-called 'static efficiency' gain (Bohm and Russell, 1985).

A further benefit from incentive-based environmental regulation is that it may accelerate innovation in abatement technologies. This 'dynamic efficiency' gain comes from the fact that with incentive-based regulation, polluters face a permanent incentive to search for additional low-cost abatement measures, which would reduce the tax payments they make on their remaining emissions.

The optimal externality tax on polluting emissions in an otherwise undistorted economy should be set at the level of the marginal external damage (MED) from the emissions. Where this tax is to be applied to a polluting consumption good, it will have the effect of reducing consumption of the good to the level where the marginal private cost plus the marginal external damage occurring at the optimal level of consumption equals the marginal benefit of private consumption.

In practice, price-based forms of regulation are frequently introduced into a context where there is already extensive direct regulation, supplementing rather than replacing this regulation. This raises the question of whether there are merits in employing multiple regulatory instruments, and about the properties of environmental taxes and other forms of price-based regulation in a context where they co-exist with direct regulation. It will not always be the case that regulatory effectiveness is enhanced by the addition of further instruments; indeed, there are examples where some instruments can undermine the effectiveness of others. For example, a stringent quantity limit on emissions can make an emissions tax redundant. One important situation where use of multiple instruments can achieve a better outcome than a single instrument is when the regulator faces uncertainty about the marginal costs of pollution abatement. Then, a mix of price and quantity regulation may perform better than a single regulatory approach (Roberts and Spence, 1976). Some of the issues raised by multiple instrument use are discussed by Christiansen and Smith (2012), including the question of the interaction between two instruments: when direct regulation is tightened, for example, does this always imply a reduction in the optimal externality tax?

Turning to the design of environmental taxes, these could take the form of taxes charged on directly measured emissions. In this case, the incentive to change behaviour is precisely and accurately targeted to the environmental problem, but substantial costs may be incurred in emissions measurement. In practice, there have been rather few such taxes; the best-known is the long-established Swedish tax on industrial emissions of nitrogen oxides (NOx) introduced in 1992 to combat environmental acidification (Millock and Sterner, 2004; OECD, 2013).

Much more commonly, taxes have been used to stimulate 'green' behaviour through changes to the structure of existing taxes on polluting commodities. How effective such initiatives are depends on how accurately the sale of the goods acts as a proxy for the environmental damage. The choice between taxing measured emissions or increasing taxes on the sale of polluting commodities is likely to reflect a trade-off between more accurate targeting and savings in tax administration and compliance costs if environmental taxes can be implemented through the existing commodity tax system. The latter, indirect, way of implementing environmental taxes raises questions about how a structure of commodity tax rates designed for efficient revenue raising should be modified to take account of the environmental costs associated with certain commodities. Sandmo (1975) analyses this issue, looking at optimal commodity taxation in a model where the consumption of one commodity generates a negative externality that is a function of total consumption of that good across all consumers. Where the government has a revenue requirement, to be met through commodity taxation, Sandmo shows that the resulting second-best tax system would have two interesting properties. First, the marginal social damage associated with consumption of the externality-generating good should only affect the tax rate for that commodity, and should not lead to any change to the taxation of complements and substitutes for the dirty good. Second, the total rate of tax to be applied to the dirty good is the weighted sum of two components, one of which reflects the marginal social damage from its consumption, and the other the conventional inverse-elasticity term governing the efficiency cost of taxation. The weighting of these two elements is governed by the marginal rate of substitution between private and public income, and hence the relative importance of the revenue requirement in determining the tax rate.

A number of papers then consider cases where the externality cannot be exactly proxied by consumption of a single commodity. Where consumption and environmental harm are more loosely linked, there may well be a case for broadening the scope of environmental taxation to include changes to the taxation of substitutes and complements for the polluting good (Diamond, 1973; Green and Sheshinski, 1976; Sandmo, 1976).

The value of environmental taxes as revenue-raising instruments came to high prominence during the 1990s. In a discussion of tax policy and climate change, Pearce (1991) contended that using the revenue raised from a carbon tax, to reduce the rates of existing taxes would constitute an additional benefit of carbon pricing, over and above its merits as an instrument of environmental policy. This 'double dividend' argument rapidly attracted considerable political attention, with advocates of green taxation arguing that such measures would also facilitate desirable fiscal reform. However, in an influential paper, Bovenberg and de Mooij (1994) investigated the relationship between environmental taxation and the distortionary effects of the existing tax system, and argued that environmental taxes would 'typically exacerbate, rather than alleviate, preexisting tax distortions – even if revenues are employed to cut preexisting distortionary taxes'. Their model is one in which household utility is a function of two public goods: public consumption and environmental quality; and three private goods: leisure, and 'clean' and 'dirty' consumption goods. The two taxes available are a linear tax on labour incomes and an *ad valorem* tax on the dirty consumption good. They explore the effects of a revenue-neutral change in the tax revenue mix, with government spending held constant. They show that, as the tax rate on the dirty commodity is increased, and the tax rate on labour income reduced, the real after-tax wage declines, increasing the distortion in the labour market. The intuition is straightforward: if the reduction in the tax on labour income had been financed by a uniform tax rate on both consumption goods, the tax shift would have been neutral in its effects on after tax wages and the labour market. However, confining the tax to the dirty consumption good alone leads to an erosion of the base of the environmental tax, through substitution towards the clean consumption good, so that the revenue available to finance the cut in the labour income tax is insufficient to offset the adverse effect of the environmental tax on after-tax wages.

Subsequent literature has explored the sensitivity of the conclusions to the underlying assumptions of the model, such as, for example, the assumed separability between environmental quality and private consumption (e.g. Schwartz and Repetto, 2000). Other papers have considered the implications of different labour market conditions (e.g. Bovenberg and van der Ploeg, 1996; Koskela and Schöb, 1999).

Pirttilä and Tuomala (1997) explore the implications of externality taxation for optimal commodity taxation in the Atkinson and Stiglitz (1976) context where the revenue instruments include a non-linear income tax. They use the two-type Mirrlees mixed taxation model with linear commodity taxes and a non-linear income tax, optimized subject to a self-selection constraint. They show that if environmental quality and leisure are complements, environmental deterioration reduces the severity of the self-selection constraint, and thus partly mitigates the required tax rate. The additivity property identified by Sandmo (1975) is found also to hold in this model, and Pirttilä and Tuomala set out separability conditions under which the externality component of the commodity tax should be set equal to the first-best Pigou-Samuelson externality tax. The same tax setting is analysed in Cremer et al. (2001), while the case with heterogeneous consumers is explored by Cremer et al. (2003). Allcott et al. (2019) includes the conceivable case where the consumption of the externality-generating good reveals information about the consumers' skill levels, assumed to impact demand beyond the effect via income.

One result highlighted by Bovenberg and de Mooij (1994) is that the fiscal costs of environmental policy interventions become more severe, the more distortionary the existing tax system. Fullerton and Metcalf (2001) note that this observation applies to a considerably wider range of policy instruments than just environmental taxes. Emissions trading has a similar effect, regardless of whether allowances are auctioned or distributed for free, and so too would certain forms of non-revenue-raising conventional regulation. In each case, the question is whether regulation increases the price of the polluting commodity to consumers (hence reducing real wages), and this effect will generally arise whenever environmental regulation creates scarcity, and where this scarcity increases the cost of marginal output.

Parry (1995) sets out a useful framework for considering the revenue aspects of environmental policy measures, decomposing the benefits from policy into three components: gross abatement benefits (before fiscal effects), revenue recycling effect, and tax interaction effect.

Non-revenue-raising environmental policy measures, such as emissions trading with grandfathered (free) allowance allocations, forego the revenue recycling effect, while nonetheless still experiencing the tax interaction effect, where the distortionary costs of existing taxes are increased when output prices rise, and hence real wages are reduced.

In general, the claim that there is a fiscal 'double dividend' from environmental tax reform has been controversial. However, one aspect of this literature has very clear policy implications. Where existing taxes involve significant marginal excess burdens, there will be a substantial benefit to using any revenues raised from environmental taxes to reduce the rates of existing taxes, rather than returning them to taxpayers in the form of a lump-sum transfer. Goulder's (1995) choice of the term 'weak double dividend' to characterize this result might suggest that it is of little significance, but in fact it has become clear that it has direct practical relevance to a major issue in the application of market mechanisms in environmental policy, namely the choice whether to auction emissions trading allowances or distribute them for free. Some calculations for hypothetical carbon pricing in the United States by Parry (2003) suggest that the economic value of the foregone revenue if allowances are distributed for free could be an order of magnitude larger than the other costs and benefits of abatement.

The major environmental externality most obviously amenable to the taxation approach is the contribution of fossil fuel use to global climate change. Combustion of fossil fuels is the largest source of man-made emissions of carbon dioxide, and emissions of CO_2 are directly linked to the carbon content of the fuels used. Taxation of fuel inputs to combustion processes in proportion to carbon content – a 'carbon tax' – provides a close proxy for taxation of the subsequent CO_2 emissions from combustion as long as no technology for carbon capture and storage is widely used.

Definition of the tax base for a carbon tax is in principle straightforward. However, determination of the efficient tax rate is more complex, reflecting the uncertainty and complex dynamics involved in the relationship between emissions and climate change. Greenstone et al. (2013) report the results of an exercise conducted by a US government inter-agency working group to assess the social cost of carbon – in other words, the marginal cost of the climate effects of a tonne of carbon emitted at the current date. Given the dynamics generated by the long persistence of CO_2 emissions in the global atmosphere (a half-life of about 100 years) and the likely changes over time in marginal abatement costs (Gillingham and Stock, 2018) optimal policy is likely to require a changing profile of carbon tax rates over time. Ulph et al. (1991) and Sinclair (1992) discuss whether an optimal carbon tax should rise or fall over time, taking account of the effect of the time profile of carbon tax rates on the time profile of depletion of fossil fuel resources, an issue also highlighted by Sinn (2007).

Countries have made different choices between carbon taxes and emissions trading. Under certainty the effects of taxes and emissions trading are largely equivalent. However, where there is uncertainty about marginal abatement costs, there is considerable significance to the choice between a tax instrument that operates by fixing the price for emissions, with an uncertain emissions outcome, and an emission trading regime that places a cap on total emissions, but faces uncertainty about the allowance price, and hence about the abatement costs that could be incurred. As Weitzman (1974) demonstrates, intervention in the form of a fixed emissions price will involve lower expected inefficiency than a tradeable permit regime with a fixed emissions cap if the slope of the marginal abatement cost schedule is steeper than the slope of the marginal damage cost schedule. By contrast, quantity regulation will be preferable if the marginal damage cost schedule is relatively steeper. Roberts and Spence (1976) show that under uncertainty, either form of intervention would be outperformed by a mixed regime in which an emissions trading system was supplemented by ceiling and floor prices, which would trigger additional allowance supply or allowance repurchases.

Road transport involves a number of distinct externalities – environmental externalities including effects on climate change as well as air pollution, noise and other local environmental effects, congestion and accident externalities, and an externality in the form of collectively borne costs arising from the uncharged marginal costs of road infrastructure damage by vehicle users. A mixture of taxes, and possibly subsidies, including fuel taxes, taxes on vehicle (characteristics), congestion charges, etc., are needed to approximate the marginal externality costs arising from individual road transport choices and to accelerate diffusion of less-polluting vehicles and the scrapping of dirty vehicles (Bento et al., 2009). Fullerton and West (2002, 2010) discuss how taxes on vehicles and motor fuels could be combined to approximate the effect of an ideal but technologically infeasible tax on measured vehicle emissions, and Parry et al. (2007) discuss the potential for other instrument combinations to encourage other environmentally desirable responses. Finely differentiated congestion charging may require adoption of technological innovations.

A complex mixture of issues also underlies the use of taxes and other instruments to regulate the externalities associated with waste management (Palmer and Walls, 1997). Waste management is costly. Ideally one would wish to confront consumers with the costs of end-of-life disposal for the products they have purchased and consumed, but in practice waste disposal

charges and taxes have tended to be a very blunt instrument, rarely differentiated according to the characteristics of waste, and frequently subsumed in more
general municipal household taxes (Kinnaman, 2006). A significant constraint
on efficient charging for waste collection and disposal is the risk of encouraging
undesirable responses, such as fly-tipping, etc. An alternative approach, which
avoids this risk, would be for end-of-life waste management costs to be reflected
in an 'advance disposal fee', a tax charged on initial purchase of certain
commodities.

7.2 Excise Taxes on Alcohol and Tobacco

Very high sales taxes on alcohol and tobacco products are levied by many
countries, often with the explicit intention of changing consumption
behaviour.[20] Most excise duties are levied as a specific rather than *ad valorem*
tax, in terms of physical metrics such as volume, weight, quantity, etc. Thus,
for example, alcoholic drinks are commonly subject either to a tax per litre of
product, or per litre of alcohol content. Tobacco products may be taxed either
on the basis of some measure of quantity, such as a tax per 100 cigarettes, or
based on the weight of tobacco contained in the product. However, in EU
countries, the cigarette excise includes an *ad valorem* element in the excise
duty, based on the anticipated or declared selling price, as well as a specific tax
per cigarette. VAT is generally imposed as well as the excise duty, and is
charged on the price inclusive of the excise duty.

The high rates of tax on these products probably have their origins in the
ability of the revenue authorities to control production and distribution (through
licensing arrangements, etc.), at a time when the imposition and effective
enforcement of more general sales taxes on a much wider set of goods and
services would have been impracticable. More recently, however, with the
availability of powerful general sales taxes such as the VAT, the revenue case
for using excise taxes on a few goods has come under scrutiny, and more
complex arguments relating to externalities or other consequences of harmful
consumption have been made to justify the retention of these excises.

While consumption of tobacco and alcohol has some clearly undesirable
effects, not all of these count as external costs, and the definition and measurement of externalities relating to consumption of these products is far from
straightforward.

In the case of alcohol and tobacco consumption, the relevant externalities
arise from

---

[20] An overview of the economic issues raised by the excise tax on tobacco can be found in Cnossen
and Smart (2005), while alcohol taxes are discussed by Smith (2005).

- the direct harm to individuals other than the consumers themselves, such as the adverse health effects of passive smoking, or the physical harm caused to others as a result of alcohol-induced violence and drunk driving;
- the harm to the consumers themselves, to the extent that it imposes costs on others that the consumers ignore in their consumption choices. A major component in these costs is typically the burden of collectively funded healthcare costs arising from illnesses caused by smoking and drinking. Other costs include the tax revenue foregone due to any loss of earnings as a result of illness or incapacity, and the reduced productivity at work of excessive drinkers, to the extent that this is not reflected in proportionately lower wages or career prospects.

The extent to which healthcare costs involve some externality element depends on the particular institutional arrangements for financing health care costs in individual countries, and will generally be higher in systems of publicly funded healthcare than in pure insurance-based systems. Viscusi (1995) points out that the significance of public expenditure effects in the overall estimated externality from smoking makes the externality argument a rather weak basis for justifying significant taxes on smoking. While treatment of the individual smoker or drinker for the health conditions caused by their choices involves some very evident costs, the impact on other costs may be ambiguous. Many smokers may not live long enough to experience the very costly health conditions associated with old age, and the premature deaths arising from smoking may also reduce other long-term public expenditure costs – such as future public pension liabilities.

In the next section, we discuss arguments for high taxes on commodities such as alcohol and tobacco that take more explicit account of the harm experienced by the individual themselves.

7.3 Merit Goods and Consumer Rationality

When analysing the desirability of commodity taxes, economists typically regard consumers as the best judge of their own interests. While an observer might regard someone as wasting money on trivial pastimes or eating unwisely, these are choices that the individual has freely chosen to make, and we may be sceptical about the legitimacy, or wisdom, of tax policies that override these choices without extremely good reason. It is this perspective which leads to the sharp separation between harm suffered by the consumer themselves from smoking and drinking and harm suffered by others, and which sees the case for high taxes as, primarily, a means to reduce the latter, external, forms of harm.

An explicit deviation from the framework of sovereign consumers is provided by the literature on 'merit goods', where the public decision maker assigns a higher value to consumption of certain goods than individuals them-selves would do, and 'demerit goods' where the opposite is the case (e.g. Musgrave and Musgrave, 1976). These goods are rarely rigorously defined, but the category seems to include goods that are now often called sin goods, goods that consumers have imperfect information about, goods that consumers need time to learn to appreciate, goods considered immoral, and goods that for some reason decision makers have paternalistic views about. There may be a case for an intervention, but not necessarily for taxes or subsidies. For instance, in many circumstances where consumers are poorly informed, providing infor-mation may be a more efficient instrument.[21]

Besley (1988) sets up a simple model where the social planner regards the consumer to be worse off than the consumer perceives herself to be. Agents misperceive the value of a (de)merit good. This defective preference case is modelled by assuming that y units of the (de)merit good consumed by the agent is conceived of as θy 'effective' units by the social planner, where $\theta > 1$ for a merit good and $\theta < 1$ for a demerit good. To achieve the first-best allocation, one can then derive a simple tax rule prescribing a tax rate $q(1 + \tau)$, so that the tax-exclusive price q is converted to an after-tax price $q(1 + \tau)$. An alternative way to model merit good arguments was presented by Schroyen (2005).

Smoking and excessive drinking cause substantial harm to the individual smokers or drinkers themselves, and we should perhaps consider rather more closely what is involved in the argument that the consumer's own preferences should be the yardstick by which to assess the case for policy intervention. What evidence is there that consumers can properly assess the long-term costs and risks of consumption, and that they act upon this knowledge? Indeed, one might think that this is unlikely in the case of commodities that involve addiction, or that diminish judgement and self-control.

Nevertheless, there are some who maintain that individual choices regard-ing consumption of these goods cannot easily be dismissed. Individuals who choose to experiment with drugs known to be highly addictive have in some sense taken choices that lead to addiction. Becker and Murphy (1988) have explored the properties of a model of 'rational addiction', to understand how a well-informed and rational consumer might nonetheless take choices that lead to addiction. In the framework they describe, the consumer is assumed to be fully informed about the consequences of current consumption for future addiction. Such a consumer would be less willing to start smoking than if there were no risk of addiction, but might nonetheless choose to do so, in effect weighing current gratification more heavily than future consequences. A

---

[21] Information may be underprovided because it is a public good.

number of empirical papers have investigated whether choices made about potentially addictive consumption do include signs of forward-looking behaviour. In a widely cited paper, for example, Becker et al. (1994) show that addictive consumption is influenced by expected future prices of the commodity as well as its current price, suggestive evidence that consumers do not entirely disregard the costs of subsequent addiction.

More recently, some economists have begun to contest the view of the rational consumer, whose choices should be regarded as revealing their own interests, even regarding commodities that entail addiction and individual harm. Major contributions towards an alternative view have been made by Gruber (see, for example, Gruber, 2010), who argues that a key deficiency in the rational model of individual economic behaviour is any meaningful account of self-control. He points out that not only does rationality require the consumer to be fully informed about future costs and risks, and capable of assessing this information and making appropriate decisions and plans, but it is also necessary that they should have the capacity to carry these plans out. He contends that there is clear evidence that this is not the case. In a number of areas of economic activity, individuals act in ways that are inconsistent over time, and that are indicative of problems of self-control. There is for example, evidence of extreme impatience in intertemporal choices, with individuals valuing immediate benefits much more strongly than future benefits, and in particular, much more strongly than when they consider the same choice at a future date. This behaviour is more consistent with hyperbolic discounting, as developed by Laibson (1997) and O'Donoghue and Rabin (1999), than with the exponential discounting which underlies the Becker–Murphy model of rational addiction. Other evidence of the significance of self-control in relation to smoking and drinking in particular are the way in which people make use of various commitment devices to enhance self-control. Gruber and Koszegi (2001) modify the Becker–Murphy model to reflect hyperbolic intertemporal preferences. The lack of self-control in relation to addictive commodities then shows up as a substantial 'internality', in the form of harm to the consumer's future self. Gruber and Koszegi (2002) present calculations showing that this future harm could be of the order of $35 per pack of cigarettes, many times greater than the estimates of the externality per pack. Allowing for the internality of smoking could add a significant amount – using plausible parameters around $9 – to the optimal tax on a pack of cigarettes. Moreover, discouraging smoking in this way would not only improve health and other outcomes, but could be viewed as desirable by smokers themselves, to the extent they have a demand for devices that strengthen current self-control.

Allcott et al. (2019) characterize optimal internality-correcting taxes on commodities over-consumed ('sin goods') or under-consumed ('merit goods') for the reasons discussed. There are several similarities with optimization of externality-correcting taxes, but there are also major differences. A negative externality is a public bad, and its cost is borne by the whole population with individual consumers perceiving the collective bad as exogenous. The internality is a private bad, and the overconsuming agent bears the entire cost. Consequently, there are no feedback effects on demand and tax revenue. It is also emphasized that the 'sin tax' may have a progressive element where low-income people both have the largest consumption bias and are the most responsive to the tax, and hence benefit the most from taxes targeted at the biased consumption. An important contribution is to consider preference heterogeneity assuming that sin-good consumption acts as a tag for ability. As a result, a crucial term, besides the bias-correcting term in the tax formula, is the covariance of welfare weights with only the component of consumption which is driven by preference heterogeneity. It represents power of the sin tax to redistribute beyond what can be achieved through the income tax. The paper also introduces a framework for determining empirically optimal sin taxes with a soda tax as example.

8 Some Further Issues

In this section, we provide a brief overview of some further issues which have been the focus for interesting research relevant to indirect taxation.

8.1 Marginal Tax Reform

Feldstein (1975) argued that, in practice, many tax reforms are 'slow and piecemeal', making incremental changes from the existing tax system. In the wake of Feldstein's emphasis on tax reform analysis, as opposed to the tax design approach, a series of papers addressed the effects of small commodity tax reforms, often called tax perturbations, departing from an arbitrary initial situation.[22] This literature mainly addresses conditions for small changes in indirect taxes to be beneficial, either by raising the utility of a single consumer or by inducing Pareto-improving reallocations in a heterogeneous-population economy.

Dixit (1975) considered a wide range of reforms in a homogenous-population economy, allowing offsetting changes in a lump-sum tax to accompany the commodity tax reform. In the spirit of Corlett and Hague, Dixit highlights in

---

[22] We may note that the Corlett–Hague (1953) analysis, discussed in detail, was indeed a pioneering tax reform analysis that predated the surge of interest in the 70s.

particular the role of substitutes and complements. He shows that in a competitive economy with constant producer prices and an initial equilibrium with equal proportional distortions, a small change in tax rates holding commodity tax revenue constant will increase welfare if all commodities whose prices are lowered are better substitutes for the untaxable numeraire than are all those whose prices are raised. A similar result is that lowering the price of any one commodity towards its marginal cost will increase welfare if the commodity is complementary to all those with a greater proportional distortion and substitute for all others including the numeraire.

A further important issue in the (commodity) tax reform context is the relationship between a one-step reform and a reform path leading to a full optimum. An important insight is that policy changes, which appear to be steps in the right direction, but stop short of attaining the full optimum, can actually reduce welfare. An interesting question addressed in Dixit (1975) is whether repeated small changes of the kind considered can be integrated to yield the same result valid for finite changes. For this to hold, the first small change must not destroy the special feature of the reform (i.e. the crucial nature of the starting point).

Diewert (1978) and Guesnerie (1977) ask whether there exist Pareto-improving reform directions where agents are heterogeneous. They provide criteria for determining whether a given equilibrium can be improved upon in a Pareto sense through small manipulations of the tax system. Guesnerie highlights the need to know producer prices, consumption bundles, and elasticities of demand[23].

8.2 The 'Inverse Optimum Problem'

The optimal tax literature that allows for agent heterogeneity and distributional concerns needs assumptions about distributional preferences, including inequality aversion, to enable us to derive the optimal policy. A different approach is to assume that the actual policy is indeed optimal given the preferences of the political decision makers, and then use the observed policy to elicit the underlying (or implicit) preferences. Ahmad and Stern (1984) coined the term 'the inverse optimum problem' to characterize this approach.

Analyses of this kind have made use of various parts of the tax/transfer policy. Some of the first were in fact based on indirect tax policy. Christiansen and Jansen (1978) inferred from indirect consumption taxes in Norway both the implicit inequality aversion parameter and the implicit valuation of social cost

---

[23] Diewert also included supply derivatives, apparently deviating from Guesnerie's result. A reconciliation was provided by Weymark (1979).

associated with the use of certain commodities assumed to have harmful effects (petrol, alcohol, tobacco). Adopting the inverse optimum approach, Ahmad and Stern (1984) found that for Indian indirect taxes to be optimal several implicit welfare weights would have to be negative, which led to the conclusion that the tax system was not optimal and not even Pareto efficient. This finding then stimulated a search for Pareto-improving directions of tax reform. Madden (1995) used data on indirect tax rates in Ireland, distributional characteristics of various goods, and estimated demand responses to infer the implicit inequality aversion. Doing this exercise for the years 1980 and 1987 finds a mild inequality aversion in 1980.

8.3 Commodity Taxes and the Tax System as a Whole

The extent to which public revenue is derived from taxation of consumption or income is closely related to the question how to divide the tax burden between labour income and capital income. Where capital income is the return on the share of labour income saved from one period to the next, a VAT will tax only the consumed part of income in the first period while it will tax the remaining (saved) part plus the return in the second period. This is equivalent to taxing solely the labour income in the first period. The burden of the tax on the return in the second period is offset by the postponement of the tax on the saved part of income.[24] A universal income tax will tax both the entire labour income in the first period and the return on savings, the capital income, in the second period. Relying more heavily on VAT rather than on income taxation is therefore a way to shift the tax burden from capital income to labour income. An alternative way to achieve this is to introduce a Nordic dual income tax, taxing capital income more leniently than labour income.

A couple of qualifications may be in order. First, where capital has already been accumulated, raising the VAT will tax wealth by eroding its purchasing power. Second, where capital income is return on inherited wealth the VAT will tax it the same way as does a comprehensive income tax. Third, the gain from the postponement of the tax on saved income, as considered here, is determined by the interest on the deferred tax liability. Any above-normal return on savings is taxed by the VAT.

It follows from these observations that the VAT is a tax on labour income and rents. This relates it to recent discussions of a destination-based cash flow tax on corporations: see, in particular, Auerbach et al. (2017). Since a tax on the cash

---

[24] The tax rate is assumed to be uniform. Differential commodity taxation in an intertemporal context has received little attention. A rare analysis addressing this issue is Christiansen (1985).

flow is a rent tax, greater reliance on VAT combined with cutting taxes on labour will have the same impact as switching to a destination-based cash flow tax.

A tax rate on consumption that rises over time introduces an intertemporal tax differentiation. Like any tax differentiation, it induces substitution and creates distortions. As discussed in Cashin and Unayama (2016), an announced tax increase will induce substitution between nondurables, storables, and durables. An amount of nondurables may be consumed sooner. Purchases of durables may be accelerated and storage costs may be incurred in pursuit of tax savings through stockpiling. Making use of data from a preannounced tax increase in Japan, Cashin and Unayama find that the intertemporal elasticity of substitution is small.

8.4 Evasion and Commodity Taxes

Even if most of the literature on tax evasion studies misreporting of income or failure to report income earned in the shadow economy, it is widely acknowledged that indirect taxes are also evaded. Sellers of taxed commodities are supposed to remit the taxes to the government. Failure to do so can take different forms. The sellers can try to hide the entire transaction or misreport the transaction as one that is liable to no or a lower tax than the one actually carried out. Goods may be smuggled into the country or produced illegally and sold in the underground economy. (See Keen 2002.) One can produce, for instance, alcohol as a moonlighting activity. One can work reporting neither income nor sales on which VAT or other indirect taxes are due, such as services offered by carpenters or plumbers. (See, e.g., Nygård et al., 2019.) Sales of goods liable to a full VAT rate can falsely be claimed to be sales that are zero-rated (e.g. exports) or subject only to a reduced rate. (See, e.g., Keen and Smith, 2006 or the section on VAT fraud in Keen, 2007.)

Tax evasion can affect what is desirable tax design through several channels. It can affect both the income distribution and the allocative efficiency of the economy, which are premises for the tax policy. It adds tax evasion as a concern when deciding on tax policy, and it can affect the efficiency and distributional effects of various tax instruments in other respects. A conceivable case for using several tax instruments is that income escaping one tax base – for instance, income taxation – may be captured by another – for instance, VAT and excise taxes. A disadvantage is that enforcement activities have to be spread across a wider area.

There is a sparse theoretical literature on optimal indirect taxation in the presence of tax evasion.

Cremer and Gahvari (1996) incorporate tax evasion into the classical Ramsey model of optimal commodity taxes with identical consumers. Each commodity is produced by firms that evade commodity tax by underreporting their output at the risk of being detected and penalized. Each unit concealed entails a resource cost. The tax per unit is the ordinary tax on the reported fraction plus a penalty rate on the evaded amount in the case of detection. Since audits are random it is the *expected* tax-inclusive price that consumers are faced with.

The major contribution of the paper is to expose several departures from the conventional Ramsey results. The equivalence of wage and uniform commodity taxation breaks down. Uniform taxation of all goods is no longer optimal in the presence of exogenous income. The inverse elasticity rule is modified by an industry-specific evasion-induced factor.

Boadway et al. (1994) consider a two-class economy with two commodities. The government can tax both income and commodities. The key assumption of the paper is that income tax can be evaded, while evading commodity taxes is not possible. Tax evasion is assumed to be socially costly where the cost is modelled as a concealment cost incurred in order to eliminate the risk of detection. Where the government is restricted to a linear income tax and commodity taxes, it is trivial that the government should confine its use of tax instruments to commodity taxes and a lump sum tax/transfer allowing it to raise revenue and redistribute income without inducing any tax evasion. Removing this restriction, letting the income tax be non-linear, is normally more efficient, and a positive marginal tax rate is warranted. Income tax evasion becomes a concern motivating the use of non-evadable, and perhaps differentiated, commodity taxes as a supplement.

Boadway and Richter (2005) discuss optimal taxation in a homogeneous population model where income is taxed, but can be underreported at a risk of being detected and penalized. Evasion entails a social cost due to the risks facing taxpayers. Households consume two consumption goods, only one of which can be taxed, and evading the commodity tax is not possible. By assumption, making use of the commodity tax will then distort the consumption bundle but its merit is not to induce tax evasion. Whether one should levy a commodity tax is then discussed in two different penalty regimes – one in which the penalty is proportional to the income tax evaded and one in which it is proportional to hidden income. In the latter regime, and only there, is it efficient to introduce a commodity tax. One will then trade off the social costs associated with (the riskiness of) tax evasion on the one hand and the distortion of the consumption bundle with uniform commodity taxes ruled out. It turns out that, for a given penalty value, this is the welfare-superior regime.

Issues of administration, evasion, and enforcement have been a particular focus for recent literature on commodity taxes in developing countries. Emran and Stiglitz (2005) argued that the presence of a large informal sector in many developing countries, beyond the reach of the tax authorities, significantly reduces the attractiveness of tax reforms which replace trade tariffs with a broad-based commodity tax such as VAT. By contrast, Keen (2008) argues that a VAT provides a mechanism for achieving at least some effective taxation of the informal sector, by taxing its inputs. De Paula and Scheinckman (2010) point out that this feature of VAT can create a partition of the economy, with informal sector firms preferring to trade with other informal sector firms, and formal sector firms preferring to trade with other firms within the VAT system. However, the partition is not fixed, and VAT enforcement activity at one point in the chain of intermediate transactions, either upstream or downstream, can have significant implications for compliance throughout the chain.

The advent of trade in digital services has posed new enforcement challenges for tax administrations, even in a domestic context, since digital downloads may often be harder to observe than deliveries of physical goods. The services are not only delivered directly by producers of digital entertainment and information offering streaming opportunities. The delivery of many services ranging from professional advice to fortune-telling can now make use of electronic communication, so that digital delivery can involve many different services that are subject to a variety of tax rules, complicating compliance and enforcement. A crucial issue is the respective obligations of the digital platform providers and the underlying suppliers of digital services.

8.5 Political Economy Aspects

Taxpayers do not always passively adjust their economic activities to the taxes in place. Interest groups engage in various influence activities in order to instigate tax changes that are in their self-interest. Besides the social loss from devoting resources to rent-seeking, unequal lobbying strength leads to differential taxation not grounded on social concerns and results in inefficient allocations. As discussed in Dixit (1996) and Dixit et al. (1997), distortions may show up on the production side or solely as distorted consumption bundles where production efficiency is preserved.

Tax reforms aiming to broaden the tax base and diminish economic distortions are liable to encounter vigorous resistance from those enjoying tax favours. The rents accruing to specific groups are typically large and concentrated, while the costs of exemptions are widely dispersed, resulting in weaker incentives for lobbying activity by the losers. Ilzetzki (2018) discusses the tension between social efficiency and the self-interest of lobby groups. He models an economy where a tax exemption enhances the relative demand for the exempted good while the resulting inefficiencies diminish aggregate demand. The relative effect will create rents for the benefit of the interest group in question while the aggregate inefficiency will harm the population at large. Ilzetzki shows that there is a tipping point where the private cost of an unreformed inefficient tax system outweighs the benefit, even to the interest groups which are immediate beneficiaries. A broad coalition of interests may agree collectively to give up their tax exemptions. The benefits to winners are larger and the cost to each individual loser is smaller when a more ambitious base-broadening reform is envisaged. The paper therefore concludes that a 'big bang' reform, abolishing many exemptions at the same time, is preferable to a gradual piecemeal reform towards a broader tax base.

Sørensen (2007) points out that a more differentiated tax system is likely to be more conducive to influencing activities, as those who are not favoured by the existing policy will find it in their interest to invoke various arguments why they too should be eligible for reduced tax rates. A commodity tax system firmly anchored in the principle of uniform taxation will act as a bulwark against pressure for reduced rates, which, under the commitment, will require a tax cut across the board, easily seen as too costly in terms of revenue forgone. Lobbying pressure is then more easily resisted than arguments for a single sector receiving the same lenient taxation as some other already tax-favoured sector.

A more pragmatic view would be that there should be a large threshold for accepting exemptions or reduced tax rates. Hence, there should be significantly less differentiation than would strictly speaking be socially optimal, the reason being that, once differentiation beyond some minimum level is accepted, restricting it to what is socially optimal would no longer be politically feasible.

8.6 Salience

The conventional (neo-classical) analysis of commodity taxes assumes optimizing behaviour where the consumers allow for actual taxes. They are both fully informed about taxes and pay attention to taxes when choosing their consumption bundles. In modern terminology, taxes are said to be salient. Recent tax literature has questioned the realism of these assumptions. The pioneering article of Chetty et al. (2009) introduced a literature on salience providing empirical evidence that in practice consumers are inattentive to taxes when prices are quoted free of tax. How prices are announced varies across jurisdictions (states or countries) and types of taxes. While the prevailing practice in Europe is to post tax-inclusive prices, not showing tax-inclusive prices on the price tags is common in the United States. But, even there, practice is not uniform: an excise tax may be included in the posted price while a sales tax is not. To what extent the salience of taxes is an issue will then depend on how tax information is announced.

Chetty et al. (2009) undertook two empirical investigations. They introduced price tags showing both tax-inclusive and pre-tax prices for a group of taxable toiletries in a big supermarket and found a significant decline in the sales of these commodities. The strategy was to compare the 'treated' commodities (with extra price tags) with two control groups: commodities in the same aisles as the treated ones and toiletry products sold in shops in nearby cities. The second experiment exploits the fact that excises on alcoholic beverages are included on the price tag while the sales tax is only added by the cashier. By examining the demand responses to changes in prices due to changes in excises and sales taxes, respectively, one can identify the effect of salience. Also this experiment reveals an under-reaction to non-salient tax changes.[25]

A paper addressing a similar issue is Blumkin et al. (2012) where the research question is whether people suffer from some form of money illusion implying that when deciding whether to supply more labour people are more discouraged by income taxes than commodity taxes. A laboratory experiment reported in the paper suggests that they are.

Allcott et al. (2018) analyse commodity taxes in the presence of salience problems obtaining optimal tax results that are strikingly similar to earlier results in the Ramsey tradition.

Interpreting behavioural responses to non-salient taxes is not straightforward. To clarify some of the issues that arise, a bit of formal analysis is helpful. Suppose a consumer purchases quantities x and y of two commodities at the respective prices $1 + t$ and $1 + s$, where the pre-tax prices are normalized to one, and t and s denote the respective tax rates. Let the utility function be given by $U = u(x) + v(y)$. The consumer's budget constraint is $(1 + t)x + (1 + s)y = Z$ where Z is the budget available for consumption expenditures. The conventional perfect optimization implies that the consumer maximizes U subject to $(1 + t)x + (1 + s)y = Z$, requiring that, besides satisfaction of the budget constraint, $u'(x)/v'(y) = (1 + t)/(1 + s)$. The assumption in the salience literature is that the consumer is inattentive to taxes and bases the choice of consumption bundle on posted tax-exclusive prices while the choice is also feasible, that is, in the budget set (Chetty et al., 2009, p. 1166).

'Being in the budget set' might be given at least two interpretations. The consumer might misperceive prices only in the short term. In a two-period setting, the agents may underestimate prices in the first one and save too little

---

[25] A conceivable effect of limited salience is that consumers may not pay much attention to minor price changes or may not find it worthwhile to adjust consumption. Chetty (2012) discusses the implications of such 'optimization frictions' for estimated demand responses.

(borrow too much). Realizing the error when entering the second period, the consumer will then have to cut back the consumption expenditure in the second period to satisfy the intertemporal budget constraint. There is even evidence that the salience problem persists even in the long run (Chetty et al., 2009, p. 1147). Then it seems that to reconcile inattention and feasibility the consumer must be assumed to neglect any tax effect on relative prices while taking account of the tax effect on the absolute price level. We can assume that the consumer maximizes U subject to a budget constraint $x + y = Z^*$, where Z^* is a real income perception of the consumer that is compatible with feasibility. The behavioural conditions are then $u'(x) = v'(y)$ and $x + y = Z^*$. We denote the resulting bundle by x^*, y^*. Given the taxes actually in place, feasibility requires that $(1 + t)x + (1 + s)y = Z$, which together with $u'(x) = v'(y)$ determines the choice of consumption bundle x^*, y^*. Z^* is then determined by $Z^* = x^* + y^*$. It follows that if $t = s$, $Z^* = Z/(1 + t)$. Then the perfect optimization is realised even in the absence of salience.

9 Directions for Future Research

Obtaining deeper insights into the effects of commodity taxes and their role as policy instruments requires further steps in theoretical, empirical as well as policy-oriented, applied research.

The most conspicuous gap in the literature on optimal commodity taxation is the relative paucity of empirical evidence on the key questions prompted by the theoretical literature. Given the centrality of quasi-separability to the question of whether commodity taxes should be uniform or differentiated, it would be clearly desirable to have more evidence about whether and to what extent this condition holds in practice. The work of Browning and Meghir (1991) provides an indication that it is very unlikely to hold, but further work along similar lines would be valuable in strengthening the research evidence about this key question. Where commodity taxes should optimally be differentiated, the natural question then arises as to what the optimal pattern of tax rates would look like: which commodities should, optimally, be taxed more heavily, and how far do the optimal tax rates deviate from uniformity? Many available estimates of elasticities are based on estimation methods which, in effect, constrain the relationship between labour supply and commodity demands in various ways, and computing the optimal pattern of tax rates without relying on estimates that depend on untested restrictions remains a challenging task.

The literature on the grouping of commodities for the purposes of taxation (line-drawing) has approached this difficult issue from a number of different directions. Each sheds interesting light on the trade-offs that arise when administrative limitations mean that only a limited number of tax rates can be employed. There remain, however, many questions to which it would be interesting to have answers. Among them are questions about optimal commodity grouping in contexts where commodities are associated with pollution or other externalities, including cases where the externality varies widely between different producers or consumers, or between production or consumption in different contexts. There are also cases where the choices made in grouping commodities may have effects on the extent of evasion, on the incentive to substitute inefficient household labour for paid services, or on the effective tax rate applying to VAT-exempt goods.

Turning to tax incidence, we note that while there is a rich theoretical literature on tax incidence and other effects of commodity taxes, there is also scope for further sophistication along various lines such as including asymmetric information and uncertainty in oligopoly models, the role of bargaining power, and agent heterogeneity as suggested by Weyl and Fabinger (2013).

The research on incidence theory and the more recent and rapidly growing empirical research on incidence seem to have evolved along rather separate lines. Bringing the two strands of research together, it is not immediately clear how well they match. The broad picture is that both theory and empirics yield a large variety of results, as expected if actual markets reflect the variety of forms addressed in theory. This does not mean that all empirical results are easily reconciled with theory. In particular, standard theory does not readily explain the observed asymmetry of responses to tax cuts and tax increases. We should also acknowledge that theories are rather general and may not capture all circumstances of relevance in each case. Specifically, the theories address anonymous transactions whereas a number of services are delivered by small businesses in a setting where personal relations may be involved. Both customer loyalty and customer reactions to price changes can matter. Exploring to what extent empirical findings are in line with theory requires a scrutiny of the strategic market situation in each case and is beyond the scope of our Element. We confine ourselves to note that bridging gaps between theory and empirical analysis of tax incidence seems to be a promising research agenda.

In a more practical policy-oriented context, we observe that various societal objectives are sometimes invoked as arguments for certain commodity tax favours (exemptions and reduced rates). Examples are regional policy, media and cultural concerns, and the importance of transport networks. A key question is whether such indirect tax policy is justified on social grounds or whether other instruments are better targeted and socially more efficient. More generally, commodity tax exemptions may have been an under-researched issue both when claimed to be socially desirable and where taxation of certain goods is considered to be administratively impracticable. Specifically, this has been an issue concerning taxation of financial services, which seems to be a field where the research community is not fully aligned.

The availability of extensive datasets on individuals and firms in many countries has opened up an increasingly productive empirical research agenda in many areas of economics, and tax policy is no exception. The combination of extensive microdata with the development of new empirical methods, such as those exploiting discontinuities (or 'notches') in the tax treatment of closely similar commodities or taxpayers, has contributed to an accelerating pace of empirical work estimating behavioural responses to various features of the tax system. Also, empirical research relevant to commodity taxation is emerging in many areas of applied literature, including literatures on IO and firm organization, the role of rationality, psychological and social factors in individual decision-making and consumer behaviour, the broader literature on tax evasion, the empirical literature on the role of the informal economy in economic development, and work modelling the endogenous determination of public policies in contexts where governments are engaged in policy competition. Increasingly, our understanding of the trade-offs involved in making better tax policy can and should be informed not only by theory, but by an extensive body of empirical research contributing rigorous evidence on the key magnitudes and behavioural responses relevant to optimal commodity tax policy choices.

Appendix

Derivation of first order conditions

This Appendix shows details of the derivation of the first-order conditions reported in Section 2.1.

$$\lambda^1 + \lambda^2 - 2\mu + \mu(m_1 + m_2) = 0$$

$$\Lambda^1 + \Lambda^2 - 2 + (m_1 + m_2) = 0$$

$$-\lambda^1 x_1^1 - \lambda^2 x_1^2 + \mu\left(X_1 - t_1 x_1^1 \frac{\partial x_1^1}{\partial y^1} - t_2 x_1^1 \frac{\partial x_2^1}{\partial y^1} - t_1 x_1^2 \frac{\partial x_1^2}{\partial y^2} - t_2 x_1^2 \frac{\partial x_2^2}{\partial y^2} \right.$$
$$\left. + t_1 S_{11} + t_2 S_{21} \right) = 0$$

$$-\lambda^1 x_2^1 - \lambda^2 x_2^2 + \mu\left(X_2 - t_1 x_2^1 \frac{\partial x_1^1}{\partial y^1} - t_2 x_2^1 \frac{\partial x_2^1}{\partial y^1} - t_1 x_2^2 \frac{\partial x_1^2}{\partial y^2} - t_2 x_2^2 \frac{\partial x_2^2}{\partial y^2} + t_1 S_{12} \right.$$
$$\left. + t_2 S_{22} \right) = 0$$

$$\lambda^1 + \lambda^2 - 2\mu + \mu t_1 \frac{\partial x_1^1}{\partial y^1} + \mu t_2 \frac{\partial x_2^1}{\partial y^1} + \mu t_1 \frac{\partial x_1^2}{\partial y^2} + \mu t_2 \frac{\partial x_2^2}{\partial y^2} = 0$$

$$-\Lambda^1 \frac{x_1^1}{X_1} - \Lambda^2 \frac{x_1^2}{X_1} + 1 - t_1 \frac{x_1^1}{X_1}\frac{\partial x_1^1}{\partial y^1} - t_2 \frac{x_1^1}{X_1}\frac{\partial x_2^1}{\partial y^1} - t_1 \frac{x_1^2}{X_1}\frac{\partial x_1^2}{\partial y^2} - t_2 \frac{x_1^2}{X_1}\frac{\partial x_2^2}{\partial y^2}$$
$$+ \frac{t_1}{q_1}\frac{S_{11}}{X_1} q_1 + \frac{t_2}{q_2}\frac{S_{12}}{X_1} q_2 = 0$$

$$-\Lambda^1 \frac{x_2^1}{X_2} - \Lambda^2 \frac{x_2^2}{X_2} + 1 - t_1 \frac{x_2^1}{X_2}\frac{\partial x_1^1}{\partial y^1} - t_2 \frac{x_2^1}{X_2}\frac{\partial x_2^1}{\partial y^1} - t_1 \frac{x_2^2}{X_2}\frac{\partial x_1^2}{\partial y^2} - t_2 \frac{x_2^2}{X_2}\frac{\partial x_2^2}{\partial y^2}$$
$$+ \frac{t_1}{q_1}\frac{S_{21}}{X_2} q_1 + \frac{t_2}{q_2}\frac{S_{22}}{X_2} q_2 = 0$$

$$\frac{t_1}{q_1}(\sigma_{11} + \sigma_{22} + \sigma_{20}) - \frac{t_2}{q_2}(\sigma_{22} + \sigma_{11} + \sigma_{10})$$

$$+ \Lambda^1 \left(\frac{x_2^1}{X_2} - \frac{x_1^1}{X_1} \right) - \Lambda^2 \left(\frac{x_1^2}{X_1} - \frac{x_2^2}{X_2} \right) + m^1 \left(\frac{x_2^1}{X_2} - \frac{x_1^1}{X_1} \right) - m^2 \left(\frac{x_1^2}{X_1} - \frac{x_2^2}{X_2} \right) = 0$$

Making use of the fact that

$$\frac{x_2^1}{X_2} + \frac{x_2^2}{X_2} = \frac{x_1^1}{X_1} + \frac{x_1^2}{X_1} = 1$$

and hence

$$\frac{x_2^1}{X_2} - \frac{x_1^1}{X_1} = \frac{x_1^2}{X_1} - \frac{x_2^2}{X_2},$$

we obtain

$$\frac{t_1}{q_1}(\sigma_{11} + \sigma_{22} + \sigma_{20}) - \frac{t_2}{q_2}(\sigma_{22} + \sigma_{11} + \sigma_{10})$$

$$+ \Lambda^1 \left(\frac{x_2^1}{X_2} - \frac{x_1^1}{X_1} \right) - \Lambda^2 \left(\frac{x_2^1}{X_2} - \frac{x_1^1}{X_1} \right) + m^1 \left(\frac{x_2^1}{X_2} - \frac{x_1^1}{X_1} \right) - m^2 \left(\frac{x_2^1}{X_2} - \frac{x_1^1}{X_1} \right) = 0$$

$$\frac{t_1}{q_1}(\sigma_{11} + \sigma_{22} + \sigma_{20}) - \frac{t_2}{q_2}(\sigma_{22} + \sigma_{11} + \sigma_{10})$$

$$+ (\Lambda^1 - \Lambda^2)\left(\frac{x_2^1}{X_2} - \frac{x_1^1}{X_1} \right) + (m^1 - m^2)\left(\frac{x_2^1}{X_2} - \frac{x_1^1}{X_1} \right) = 0$$

$$\left[\frac{t_1}{q_1}(\sigma_{11} + \sigma_{22} + \sigma_{20}) - \frac{t_2}{q_2}(\sigma_{22} + \sigma_{11} + \sigma_{10}) \right] + (\Lambda^1 - \Lambda^2)\left(\frac{x_2^1}{X_2} - \frac{x_1^1}{X_1} \right)$$

$$+ (m^1 - m^2)\left(\frac{x_2^1}{X_2} - \frac{x_1^1}{X_1} \right) = 0.$$

References

Agrawal, D. R. (2015). The tax gradient: Spatial aspects of fiscal competition. *American Economic Journal: Economic Policy*, **7**, 1–29.

Agrawal, D. R. (2017). *The Internet as a Tax Haven? The Effect of the Internet on Tax Competition*. http://dx.doi.org/10.2139/ssrn.2328479

Ahmad, E., & Stern, N. (1984). The theory of reform and the Indian indirect taxes. *Journal of Public Economics*, **25**, 25–8.

Allcott, H., Lockwood, B. B., & Taubinsky, D. (2018). Ramsey strikes back: Optimal commodity taxes and redistribution in the presence of salience. *AEA Papers and Proceedings*, **108**, 88–92.

Allcott, H., Lockwood, B. B., & Taubinsky, D. (2019). Regressive sin taxes, with an application to the optimal soda tax. *The Quarterly Journal of Economics*, **134**, 1557–626.

Atkinson, A. B., & Stiglitz, J. E. (1976). The design of tax structure: Direct versus indirect taxation. *Journal of Public Economics*, **6**, 55–75.

Auerbach, A. J., & Gordon, R. H. (2002). Taxation of financial services under a VAT. *American Economic Review*, **92**, 411–16.

Auerbach, A. J., Devereux, M., Keen, M., & Vella, J. (2017). *Destination-Based Cash Flow Taxation*. Oxford: Saïd Business School.

Bargain, O., & Donni, O. (2014). Optimal commodity taxation and redistribution within households. *Economica*, **81**, 48–62.

Barham, V., Poddar, S. N., & Whalley, J. (1987). The tax treatment of insurance under a consumption type, destination basis VAT. *National Tax Journal*, **40**, 171–81.

Bastani, S., Blomquist, S., & Pirttilä, J. (2015). Counterargument to the recommendation in the Mirrlees Review. *Oxford Economic Papers*, **67**, 455–478.

Baumol, W. J. (1972). On taxation and the control of externalities. *American Economic Review*, **62**, 307–22.

Becker, G. S. (1965). A theory of the allocation of time. *Economic Journal*, **75**, 493–517.

Becker, G. S., Grossman, M., & Murphy, K. M. (1994). An empirical analysis of cigarette addiction. *American Economic Review*, **84**, 396–418.

Becker, G. S. & Murphy, K. M. (1988). A theory of rational addiction. *Journal of Political Economy*, **96**, 675–700.

Belan, P., Gauthier, S., & Laroque, G. (2008). Optimal grouping of commodities for indirect taxation. *Journal of Public Economics*, **92**, 1738–50.

Bento, A. M., Goulder, L. H., Jacobsen, M. R., & von Haefen, R. H. (2009). Efficiency and distributional impacts of increased U.S. gasoline taxes. *American Economic Review*, **99**, 667–99.

Benzarti, Y., & Carloni, D. (2019). Who really benefits from consumption tax cuts? Evidence from a large VAT reform in France. *American Economic Journal: Economic Policy*, **11**, 38–63.

Benzarti, Y., Carloni, D., Harju, J., & Kosonen, T. (2020). What goes up may not come down: Asymmetric incidence of value-added taxes. *Journal of Political Economy*, **128**, 4438–74.

Besley, T. J. (1988). A simple model for merit good arguments. *Journal of Public Economics*, **35**, 371–83.

Besley, T. J., & Rosen, H. S. (1999). Sales taxes and prices: An empirical analysis. *National Tax Journal*, **52**, 157–78.

Blumkin, T., Ruffle, B., & Ganun, Y. (2012). Are income and consumption taxes ever really equivalent? Evidence from a real-effort experiment with real goods. *European Economic Review*, **56**, 1200–19.

Boadway, R. W. (2012). *From Optimal Tax Theory to Tax Policy: Retrospective and Prospective Views*. Munich Lectures in Economics. Cambridge, MA: MIT Press.

Boadway, R., & Gahvari, F. (2006). Optimal taxation with consumption time as a leisure or labor substitute. *Journal of Public Economics*, **90**, 1851–78.

Boadway, R., & Keen, M. (2003). Theoretical perspectives on the taxation of capital income and financial services: A survey. In Honohan, P. (ed.), *Taxation of Financial Intermediation. Theory and Practice for Emerging Economies*. New York: Oxford University Press, pp. 31–80.

Boadway, R., Marchand, M., & Pestieau, P. (1994). Towards a theory of the direct-indirect tax mix. *Journal of Public Economics*, **55**, 71–88.

Boadway, R. W., & Richter, W. F. (2005). Trading off tax distortions and tax evasion. *Journal of Public Economic Theory*, 7, 361–81.

Bohm, P., & Russell, C. (1985). Comparative analysis of alternative policy instruments. In Kneese, A. V., & Sweeney, J. L. (eds.), *Handbook of Natural Resource and Energy Economics*, Vol. 1. New York: Elsevier, pp. 395–460.

Boiteux, M. (1956). Sur la gestion des monopoles publics astreints à l'équilibre budgétaire. *Econometrica*, **24**, 22–40.

Bovenberg, L. (1994), Destination- and origin-based taxation under international capital mobility. *International Tax and Public Finance*, **1**, 247–73.

Bovenberg, A. L., & de Mooij, R. (1994). Environmental levies and distortionary taxation. *American Economic Review*, **84**, 1085–9.

Bovenberg, A. L., & van der Ploeg, F. (1996). Optimal taxation, public goods and environmental policy with involuntary unemployment. *Journal of Public Economics*, **62**, 59–83.

Browning M., & Meghir, C. (1991). The effects of male and female labour supply on commodity demands. *Econometrica*, **59**, 925–51.

Büttner, T., & Erbe, K. (2014). Revenue and welfare effects of financial sector VAT exemption. *International Tax and Public Finance*, **21**, 1028–50.

Carbonnier, C. (2007). Who pays sales taxes? Evidence from French VAT reforms, 1987–1999. *Journal of Public Economics*, **91**, 1219–29.

Chetty, R. (2012). Bounds on elasticities with optimization frictions: A Synthesis of micro and macro evidence on labor supply. *Econometrica*, **80**, 969–1018.

Chetty, R., Looney, A., & Kroft, K. (2009). Salience and taxation: Theory and evidence. *American Economic Review*, **99**, 1145–77.

Christiansen, V. (1984). Which commodity taxes should supplement the income tax? *Journal of Public Economics*, **24**, 195–220.

Christiansen, V. (1985). The choice of excise taxes when savings and labour decisions are distorted. *Journal of Public Economics*, *28*, 95–110.

Christiansen, V. (1994). Cross-border shopping and the optimum commodity tax in a competitive and monopoly market. *Scandinavian Journal of Economics*, **96**, 329–41.

Christiansen, V. (2017). Indirect taxation of financial services. CESifo Working Paper Series No. 6675.

Christiansen, V. & Jansen, E. S. (1978). Implicit social preferences in the Norwegian system of indirect taxation. *Journal of Public Economics*, **10**, 217–45.

Christiansen, V., & Smith, S. (2001). The economics of duty-free shopping. CESifo Working Paper No 595.

Christiansen, V., & Smith, S. (2004). National policy interests in the duty-free market. *CESifo Economic Studies*, **50**, 351–75.

Christiansen, V., & Smith, S. (2008). Optimal commodity taxation with duty-free shopping. *International Tax and Public Finance*, **15**, 274–96.

Christiansen, V., & Smith, S. (2012). Externality-correcting taxes and regulation. *The Scandinavian Journal of Economics*, **114**, 358–83.

Cnossen, S., & Shoup, C. S. (1987), Coordination of value-added taxes. In Cnossen, S. (ed.), *Tax Coordination in the European Community*. Deventer: Kluwer, pp. 59–84.

Cnossen, S., & Smart, M. (2005). Taxation of tobacco. In Cnossen, S. (ed.), *Theory and Practice of Excise Taxation*. Oxford: Oxford University Press, pp. 21–55.

Corlett, W. J., & Hague, D. C. (1953). Complementarity and the excess burden of taxation, *Review of Economic Studies*, **21**, 21–30.

Crawford, I., Keen, M., & Smith, S. (2010). Value Added Tax and Excises. In Mirrlees, J., et al. (eds.), *Dimensions of Tax Design: The Mirrlees Review*. Oxford: Oxford University Press, pp. 275–362.

Crawford, I., & Tanner, S. (1995). Bringing it all back home: Alcohol taxation and cross-border shopping, *Fiscal Studies*, **16**, 94–114.

Cremer, H., & Gahvari, F. (1996). Tax evasion and optimal commodity taxation. *Journal of Public Economics*, **50**, 261–75.

Cremer, H., Gahvari, F., & Ladoux, N. (1998). Externalities and optimal taxation. *Journal of Public Economics*, **70**, 343–64.

Cremer, H., Gahvari, F., & Ladoux, N. (2003). Environmental taxes with heterogeneous consumers: An application to energy consumption in France. *Journal of Public Economics*, **87**, 2791–815.

Cashin, D., & Unayama, T. (2016). Measuring intertemporal substitution in consumption: Evidence from a VAT increase in Japan. *The Review of Economics and Statistics*, **98**, 285–97.

Delipalla, S., & Keen, M. (1992). The comparison between ad valorem and specific taxation under imperfect competition, *Journal of Public Economics*, **49**, 351–67.

De Paula, Á. , & Scheinkman, J. A. (2010). Value-added taxes, chain effects, and informality. *American Economic Journal: Macroeconomics*, **2**, 195–221.

Devereux, M. P., & Vella, J. (2017). Implications of Digitalization for International Corporate Tax Reform. Oxford University Centre for Business Taxation. Working Paper 17/07.

Diamond, P. (1973). Consumption externalities and imperfect corrective pricing, *Bell Journal of Economics*, **4**, 526–38.

Diamond, P., & Mirrlees, J. A. (1971). Optimal taxation and public production I: Production efficiency; II Tax rules. *American Economic Review*, **61**, 8–27 and 261–278.

Diewert, W. E. (1978). Optimal tax perturbations. *Journal of Public Economics*, **10**, 139–77.

Dixit, A. (1975). Welfare effects of tax and price changes. *Journal of Public Economics*, **4**, 103–23.

Dixit, A. (1996). Special-interest lobbying and endogenous commodity taxation. *Eastern Economic Journal*, **22**, 375–88.

Dixit, A., Grossman, G. M., & Helpman, E. (1997). Common agency and Coordination: General theory and application to government policy making. *Journal of Political Economy*, **105**, 752–69.

Dixit A. K., & Stern, N. H. (1982). Oligopoly and welfare: A unified presentation with applications to trade and development. *European Economic Review*, **19**, 123–43.

Ebrill, L., Keen, M., Bodin, J.-P., & Summers, V. (2001). *The Modern VAT*. Washington, DC: International Monetary Fund.

Edwards, J., Keen, M., & Tuomala, M. (1994). Income tax, commodity taxes and public good provision: a brief guide. *FinanzArchiv*, **51**, 472–87.

Emran, S. M., & Stiglitz, J. E. (2005). On selective indirect tax reform in developing countries. *Journal of Public Economics*, **89**, 599–623.

Feldstein, M. (1975). On the theory of tax reform. *Journal of Public Economics*, **6**, 77–104.

Fratianni, M., & Christie, H. (1981). Abolishing fiscal frontiers within the EEC. *Public Finance – Finances publiques*, **36**, 411–29.

Fullerton, D., Leicester, A., & Smith, S. (2010). Environmental taxes. In Mirrlees, J., et al. (eds.), *Dimensions of Tax Design: The Mirrlees Review*. Oxford: Oxford University Press, pp. 423–518.

Fullerton, D., & Metcalf, G. E. (2001). Environmental controls, scarcity rents, and pre-existing distortions, *Journal of Public Economics*, **80**, 249–67.

Fullerton, D., & West, S. E. (2002). Can taxes on cars and on gasoline mimic an unavailable tax on emissions? *Journal of Environmental Economics and Management*, **43**, 135–57.

Fullerton, D., & West, S. E. (2010). Tax and subsidy combinations for the control of car pollution. *The B.E. Journal of Economic Analysis & Policy*, 10: Iss. 1 (Advances), Article 8.

Gaarder, I. (2018). Incidence and distributional effects of value added taxes. *Economic Journal*, **129**, 853–76.

Gahvari, F. (2007). On optimal commodity taxes when consumption is time consuming. *Journal of Public Economic Theory*, **9**(1), 1–27.

Gahvari, F., & Yang, C. C. (1993) Optimal commodity taxation and household consumption activities *Public Finance Quarterly*, **21**, 479–87.

Gilitzer, C, Kleven, H. J., & Slemrod, J. (2017). A characteristics approach to optimal taxation: Line drawing and tax-driven product innovation. *Scandinavian Journal of Economics*, **119**, 240–67.

Gillingham, K., & Stock, J. H. (2018). The costs of reducing greenhouse gas emissions. *Journal of Economic Perspectives*, **32**, 53–72.

Goolsbee, A. (2000). In a world without borders: The impact of taxes on internet commerce. *Quarterly Journal of Economics*, 115, 561–76.

Goolsbee, A., Lovenheim, M. F., & Slemrod, J. (2010). Playing with fire: Cigarettes, taxes, and competition from the internet. *American Economic Journal: Economic Policy*, **2**, 131–54.

Gordon, J. (1989). Tax reform via commodity grouping. *Journal of Public Economics*, **39**, 67–81.

Goulder, L. H. (1995). Environmental taxation and the double dividend: A reader's guide. *International Tax and Public Finance*, **2**, 157–83.

Green, J., & Sheshinski, E. (1976). Direct versus indirect remedies for externalities. *Journal of Political Economy*, **84**, 797–808.

Greenstone, M., Kopits, E., & Wolverton, A. (2013). Developing a social cost of carbon for US regulatory analysis: A methodology and interpretation. *Review of Environmental Economics and Policy*, **7**, 23–46.

Gruber, J. (2010). Value added tax and excises: Commentary. In Mirrlees, J., et al. (eds.), *Dimensions of Tax Design: The Mirrlees Review*, Oxford: Oxford University Press, pp. 405–22.

Gruber, J., & Koszegi, B. (2001). Is addiction 'rational'? Theory and evidence. *Quarterly Journal of Economics*, **116**, 1261–303.

Gruber, J., & Koszegi, B. (2002). A theory of government regulation of addictive bads: optimal tax levels and tax incidence for cigarette excise taxation. NBER Working Paper No 8777.

Grubert, H., & Mackie, J. (2000). Must financial services be taxed under a consumption tax? *National Tax Journal*, **53**, 23–40.

Guesnerie, R. (1977). On the direction of tax reform. *Journal of Public Economics*, **7**, 179–202.

Harding M., Leibtag, E., & Lovenheim, M. (2012). The heterogenous geographic and socioeconomic incidence of cigarette taxes: Evidence from Nielsen homescan data. *American Economic Journal: Economic Policy*, **4**, 169–98.

Harju, J., Kosonen, T., & Nordström-Skans, O. (2018). Firm types, price-setting strategies, and consumption-tax incidence. *Journal of Public Economics*, **165**, 48–72.

Ilzetzki, E. (2018). Tax reform and the political economy of the tax base. *Journal of Public Economics*, **164**, 197–210.

Jack, W. (2000). The treatment of financial services under a broad-based consumption tax. *National Tax Journal*, **53**, 841–51.

Jacobs, B., & Boadway, R. (2014). Optimal linear commodity taxation under optimal non-linear income taxation. *Journal of Public Economics* **117**, 201–10.

Kanbur, R., & Keen, M. (1993). Jeux sans frontières: Tax competition and tax coordination when countries differ in size. *American Economic Review*, **83**, 877–92.

Kay, J. A., & Keen, M. J. (1983). How should commodities be taxed? Market structure, product heterogeneity and the optimal structure of commodity taxes. *European Economic Review*, **23**, 339–58.

Keen, M. (1993). The welfare economics of tax coordination in the European Community, *Fiscal Studies* **14**, 15–36.

Keen, M. (2002). Some international issues in commodity taxation, *Swedish Economic Policy Review*, **9**, 9–37.

Keen, M. (2007). VAT attacks! *International Tax and Public Finance*, **14**, 365–381.

Keen, M. (2008). VAT, tariffs, and withholding: border taxes and informality in developing countries. *Journal of Public Economics*. **92**, 1892–906.

Keen, M, & Mintz, J. (2004). The optimal threshold for a value-added tax. *Journal of Public Economics*, **88**, 559–76.

Keen, M., & Smith, S. (1996) The future of value added tax in the European Union. *Economic Policy*, **23**, 375–420.

Keen, M., & Smith, S. (2000) Viva VIVAT! *International Tax and Public Finance*, **7**, 741–51.

Keen, M., & Smith, S. (2006). VAT fraud and evasion. What do we know, and what can be done? *National Tax Journal*, **59**, 861–87.

Kinnaman, T. (2006). Policy watch: Examining the justification for residential recycling. *Journal of Economic Perspectives*, **20**, 219–32.

Kleven, H. J. (2004) Optimum taxation and the allocation of time. *Journal of Public Economics*, **88**, 545–57.

Kleven, H. J., Richter, W. F., & Sørensen, P. B. (2000). Optimal taxation with household production. *Oxford Economic Papers* **52**, 584–94.

Kneese, A. V, . & Bower, B. T. (1968). *Managing water quality. Economics, technology, institutions*. Baltimore: Johns Hopkins University Press.

Kopczuk, W., Marion, J., Muehlegger, E., & Slemrod, J. (2016) Does tax-collection invariance hold? Evasion and pass-through of state diesel taxes. *American Economic Journal: Economic Policy*, **8**. 251–86.

Koskela, E. & Schöb, R. (1999). Alleviating unemployment: The case for green tax reforms. *European Economic Review*. **43**, 1723–46.

Kosonen, T. (2015). More and cheaper haircuts after VAT cut? On the efficiency and incidence of service sector consumption taxes. *Journal of Public Economics*, **131**, 87–100.

Laibson, D. (1997). Golden eggs and hyperbolic discounting. *Quarterly Journal of Economics*, **112**, 443–77.

Lancaster, K. J. (1966). A new approach to consumer theory. *Journal of Political Economy*, **74**, 132–157.

Leal, A., López-Laborda, J., & Rodrigo, F. (2010). Cross-border shopping: A survey. *International Advances in Economic Research*, **16**, 135–48.

Lockwood, B. (2015). How should financial intermediation services be taxed? In de Mooij, R., & Nicodème, G. (eds.), *Taxation and Regulation of the Financial Sector*. Cambridge, MA: The MIT Press, pp. 133–56.

Lockwood, B., de Meza, D. & Myles, G. (1994a). When are destination and origin regimes equivalent? *International Tax and Public Finance*, **1**, 5–24.

Lockwood, B., de Meza, D., & Myles, G. (1994b). The equivalence between destination and non-reciprocal restricted origin regimes. *Scandinavian Journal of Economics*, **96**, 311–28.

Lockwood, B., & Yerushalmi, E. (2019). How should payment services be taxed? *Social Choice and Welfare*, **53**, 21–47.

Madden, D. (1995). An analysis of indirect tax reform in Ireland in the 1980s. *Fiscal Studies*, **16**, 18–37.

Meade, J. E. (1955). *Trade and Welfare*. London: Oxford University Press.

Meade Report (1978). *The Structure and Reform of Indirect Taxation: Report of a Committee chaired by Professor J. E. Meade*. London: Allen and Unwin.

Merriman, D. (2010). The micro-geography of tax avoidance: evidence from littered cigarette packs in Chicago. *American Economic Journal: Economic Policy*, **2**, 61–84.

Millock. K., & Sterner, T. (2004). NOx emissions in France and Sweden: advanced fee schemes versus regulation. In Harrington, W., Morgenstern, R. D., & Sterner, T. (eds.), *Choosing Environmental Policy: Comparing Instruments and Outcomes in the United States and Europe*. Washington, DC: Resources for the Future, pp. 117–32.

Mintz, J., & Tulkens, H. (1986). Commodity tax competition between member states of a federation: equilibrium and efficiency. *Journal of Public Economics*, **29**, 133–72.

Miravete, E., Seim, K., & Thurk, J. (2018). Market power and the Laffer curve. *Econometrica*, **86**, 1651–1687.

Musgrave, R. A., & Musgrave, P. B. (1976). *Public Finance in Theory and Practice*. New York: McGraw- Hill Book Company.

Newell, R., & Stavins, R. (2003). Cost heterogeneity and the potential savings from market-based policies. *Journal of Regulatory Economics*, **23**, 43–59.

Nielsen, S. B. (2001). A simple model of commodity taxation and cross-border shopping. *Scandinavian Journal of Economics*, **103**, 599–623.

Nygård, O. E., & Revesz, J. T. (2016). A literature review on optimal indirect taxation and the uniformity debate. *Review of Public Economics*, **218**, 107–38.

Nygård, O. E., Slemrod, J., & Thoresen, T. O. (2019). Distributional implications of joint tax evasion. *The Economic Journal*, **129**, 1894–923.

O'Donoghue, T., & Rabin, M. (1999). Doing it now or later. *American Economic Review*, **89**, 103–24.

OECD (2013). *The Swedish Tax on Nitrogen Oxide Emissions: Lessons in Environmental Policy Reform*. OECD Environmental Policy Paper No 2. Paris: Organisation for Economic Cooperation and Development.

OECD (2015). *Addressing the Tax Challenges of the Digital Economy*. Paris: Organisation for Economic Cooperation and Development.

Palmer, K., and Walls, M. (1997), Optimal policies for solid waste disposal: taxes, subsidies, and standards. *Journal of Public Economics*, **65**, 193–205.

Parry, I. (1995). Pollution taxes and revenue recycling. *Journal of Environmental Economics and Management*, **29**, 64–77.

Parry, I. (2003), Fiscal interactions and the case for carbon taxes over grand-fathered carbon permits. *Oxford Review of Economic Policy*, **19**, 385–99.

Parry, I., Walls, M., & Harrington, W. (2007). Automobile externalities and policies. *Journal of Economic Literature*, **45**, 373–99.

Pearce, D. (1991). The role of carbon taxes in adjusting to global warming. *The Economic Journal*, **101**, 938–48.

Pigou, A. C. (1920). *The Economics of Welfare*. London: Macmillan.

Pirttilä, J., & Tuomala, M. (1997). Income tax, commodity tax and environmental policy. *International Tax and Public Finance*, **4**, 379–93.

Pless J., & van Benthem, A. A. (2019). Pass-through as a test for market power: An application to solar subsidies. *American Economic Journal: Applied Economics*, **11**, 367–401.

Ramsey, F. (1927). A contribution to the theory of taxation. *Economic Journal*, **37**, 47–61.

Roberts, M. J., & Spence, M. (1976). Effluent charges and licenses under uncertainty. *Journal of Public Economics*, **5**, 193–208.

Saez, E. (2002) The desirability of commodity taxation under non-linear income taxation and heterogeneous tastes. *Journal of Public Economics*, **83**, 217–30.

Sandmo, A. (1975). Optimal taxation in the presence of externalities. *Swedish Journal of Economics*, **77**, 86–98.

Sandmo, A. (1976). Direct versus indirect Pigovian taxation. *European Economic Review*, **7**, 337–49.

Sandmo, A. (1990). Tax distortions and household production. *Oxford Economic Papers*, **42**, 78–90.

Sandmo, A. (1995). Public finance and the environment. In Bovenberg, L. & Cnossen, S. (eds.), *Public Economics and the Environment in an Imperfect World*. Dordrecht: Kluwer, pp. 19–35.

Sandmo, A. (2000). *The Public Economics of the Environment*. Oxford: Oxford University Press.

Schroyen, F. (2005). An alternative way to model merit good arguments. *Journal of Public Economics*, **89**, 957–66.

Schwarz, J., & Repetto, R. (2000). Nonseparable utility and the double dividend debate: Reconsidering the tax interaction effect. *Environmental and Resource Economics*, **15**, 149–57.

Seade, J. (1985). Profitable Cost Increases and the Shifting Of Taxation: Equilibrium Response of Markets in Oligopoly. Warwick Economic Research Papers No. 260.

Shibata, H. (1967), The theory of economic unions: A comparative analysis of customs unions, free trade areas and tax unions. In Shoup, C. S. (ed.), *Fiscal Harmonisation in Common Markets*. New York: Columbia University Press, pp. 145–264.

Sinclair, P. (1992), High does nothing and rising is worse: carbon taxes should keep declining to cut harmful emissions, *The Manchester School*, **60**, 41–52.

Sinn, H.-W. (2007), *Public Policies Against Global Warming*, CESifo Working Paper 2087, Munich: CESifo.

Smith, S. (2005). Economic issues in alcohol taxation. In Cnossen, S. (ed.), *Theory and Practice of Excise Taxation*. Oxford: Oxford University Press, pp. 56–83.

Sørensen, P. B. (2007). The theory of optimal taxation: what is the policy relevance? *International Tax and Public Finance*, 14, 383–406.

Stern, N. (1982). Optimum taxation with errors in administration. *Journal of Public Economics*, **17**, 181–211.

Stern, N. (1987). The effects of taxation, price control and government contracts in oligopoly and monopolistic competition. *Journal of Public Economics*, **32**, 133–58.

Stiglitz, J. (1982). Self-selection and Pareto efficient taxation. *Journal of Public Economics*, **17**, 213–40.

Ulph, A., Ulph, D., & Pezzey, J. (1991). Should a Carbon Tax Rise or Fall over Time? University of Bristol, Department of Economics, Discussion Paper No 91/309.

Viscusi, W. K. (1995). Cigarette taxation and the social consequences of smoking. *Tax Policy and the Economy*, **9**, 51–101.

Weitzman, M. L. (1974). Prices versus quantities. *Review of Economic Studies*, **41**, 477–91.

Weyl, E. G., and Fabinger, M. (2013). Pass-through as an economic tool: Principles of incidence under imperfect competition. *Journal of Political Economy*, **121**, 528–83.

Weymark, J. A. (1979). A reconciliation of recent results in optimal taxation theory. *Journal of Public Economics*, **12**, 171–89.

Wilson, J. D. (1989). On the optimal tax base for commodity taxation. *American Economic Review*, **79**, 1196–206.

Acknowledgements

We gratefully acknowledge the helpful comments we have received from an anonymous referee and from Chris Heady, and the advice we have received from the editors Robin Boadway and Chiara Del Bo.

Public Economics

Robin Boadway
Queen's University
Robin Boadway is Emeritus Professor of Economics at Queen's University. His main research interests are in public economics, welfare economics and fiscal federalism.

Frank A. Cowell
The London School of Economics and Political Science
Frank A. Cowell is Professor of Economics at the London School of Economics. His main research interests are in inequality, mobility and the distribution of income and wealth.

Massimo Florio
University of Milan
Massimo Florio is Professor of Public Economics at the University of Milan. His main interests are in cost-benefit analysis, regional policy, privatization, public enterprise, network industries and the socio-economic impact of research infrastructures.

About the series
This Cambridge Elements series in Public Economics provides authoritative and up-to-date reviews of core topics and recent developments in the field. It includes state-of-the-art contributions on all areas in the field. The editors are particularly interested in the new frontiers of quantitative methods in public economics, experimental approaches, behavioral public finance, and empirical and theoretical analysis of the quality of government and institutions.

Public Economics

Elements in the series

A full series listing is available at: www.cambridge.org/ElePubEcon

CPSIA information can be obtained
at www.ICGtesting.com
Printed in the USA
LVHW010931040821
694404LV00013B/984